WITCH FUGITIVE

WITCH FUGITIVE

SCHOOL OF NECESSARY MAGIC RAINE CAMPBELL™
BOOK 06

JUDITH BERENS MARTHA CARR MICHAEL ANDERLE

DISRUPTIVE IMAGINATION®

LMBPN Publishing
PMB 196, 2540 South Maryland Pkwy
Las Vegas, NV 89109

First US edition, April 2019

Thanks to the JIT Readers

Nicole Emens
Misty Roa
Diane L. Smith
Micky Cocker
Jeff Eaton
Larry Omans
Daniel Weigert

If we've missed anyone, please let us know!

Editor
The Skyhunter Editing Team

DEDICATIONS

From Martha

To everyone who still believes in magic
and all the possibilities that holds.
To all the readers who make this
entire ride so much fun.
And to my son, Louie and so many wonderful friends who
remind me all the time of what
really matters and how wonderful
life can be in any given moment.

From Michael

To Family, Friends and
Those Who Love
To Read.
May We All Enjoy Grace
To Live The Life We Are
Called.

Paranormal Defense Agent Watson raised his wand as he narrowed his eyes on the small, weathered office building. A badly faded yellow sign in front declared **COMMERCIAL SPACE FOR RENT**. It also offered a now useless phone number. As far as the PDA could discern, the building was technically without an owner—or, at least, one who was alive. It'd slipped through the cracks of multiple company bankruptcies and general legal confusion.

The loose garbage strewn around the outside and several shattered windows proved that no one had rented any of the office spaces for a long time. The location was merely another casualty of the chaotic times that accompanied the beginning of the opening of the gates to Oriceran.

"Everyone, prepare to breach," Agent Watson whispered and trusted the receiver to transmit to the gathered PDA personnel. "We have to do this right if we want to snag the target." The comms was technology in service of one of the few magic-heavy federal agencies. Sometimes, a good gadget was worth ten spells.

This was the grand irony of being a PDA agent. For all their magical ability, their targets were also magicals, which meant any use of magic could potentially be sensed and ruin a good raid. It wasn't like the old days. Even under normal circumstances, the background level and knowledge of magic possessed by rogues and criminals now made what once were trivial tasks for their predecessors difficult. Technology could help with that.

Their current target could use portal magic. They would need to seal her in before they breached, which necessitated that many agents would not able to help to directly enter and clear the building. Their task would be to maintain the spell that blocked her portals.

A witch and wizard flanked Agent Watson on either side. Both were good agents he'd worked with for years and were as eager as he was to arrest the target inside the abandoned office building. All three stood near the front door while other teams were spread out to cover every other exit. They'd even had time to study the layout before preparing for the raid. Fortunately, they already had an established protocol for apprehending this particular target.

He took a few deep breaths and his heart pounded in anticipation. Their quarry was one of the most wanted on the Department of Homeland Security's list of dangerous enhanced individuals, and she was even worse because it was hard to anticipate her actions, even under normal circumstances.

Eris was the self-declared Witch Queen of Chaos. It

didn't matter that her real name was Lisa and she'd been born in Omaha. She'd cast that identity off a long time before to embody everything associated with her chosen name—discord and chaos.

At least with normal criminals, the government could study their motivations and use that to determine where they might strike next. Eris didn't care about money, power, or influence, however. Her only motivation was to spread a message of chaos and unpredictability under the guise of freedom.

Sometimes, that resulted in nothing more than harmless pranks. At other times, it caused massive property damage and injuries—and that didn't include the times she thought it would be amusing to play a few pranks on the military. The woman displayed no intimation that she even understood how dangerous her actions were.

It wasn't like she'd always been an insane chaos witch. Her early life had been normal enough and she'd even attended a reputable government-sponsored magic school. A chance encounter with an ancient artifact had changed everything.

Agent Watson didn't care if it was the artifact's fault or if Eris had decided more power meant she could do what she wanted to whomever she wanted for whatever reasons she made up. It didn't matter. The PDA's job remained the same—to take her into custody before she could hurt anyone else.

The PDA, FBI, and Homeland Security had spent six months tracking the woman down. Her personality wasn't the only thing the artifact had changed. Tracking spells—and even magic cast using joint rituals—were useless against Eris. Her current psychological profile made it all but impossible to predict where she might strike, which forced law enforcement to spread their resources to cover all possible eventualities.

Today, though, they'd gotten lucky thanks to a few fortuitously placed police drones that happened to catch sight of her through a window. The chaos she created couldn't do much to hide her when she was caught on camera.

Agent Watson allowed himself a grin of triumph. He would lead the team that would prove why order always won over chaos in the end.

"Wands up," he commanded. "I want the suppression team to begin the portal block. It's go-time."

Magic filled the area. They had caught her by surprise. Spells pulsed from inside. Eris must have reacted to being sealed in and now lashed out in protest when she realized she was caught in the PDA net. The agent almost laughed. All that power and she was merely another criminal about to be caught because she grew too arrogant.

"Shields up," he commanded. He waited a moment to give everyone a chance to cast their defensive spells. "And breach. Go, go, go."

Loud explosions followed as each team forced their designated doors with the help of powerful spells.

Agent Watson's team hurtled inside and swung their wands strategically as they sought their target. A dusty, web-covered desk stood in the front lobby, along with a few overturned chairs and a musty green sofa. Dirty foot-prints tracked the floor.

Eris hadn't been the first person in the building. A few

seconds passed before the agent glanced over his shoulder and wondered if the front door had even been locked.

"Front lobby clear," he reported and wondered if they should have risked a few scrying spells after all. They might not have been able to track the witch directly, but that didn't mean they couldn't haven't located her while searching the building with magic.

He decided it didn't matter. She couldn't portal out, which meant she would have to go through the PDA to escape.

Other teams reported clear statuses as they swept deeper into the office building. The structure was only one story, and there was a small number of different office units, along with a decent-sized cafeteria near the center.

The team rushed forward. The PDA witch kicked an office door in as he shouldered the opposite door wide. The other wizard agent continued down the wide hallway. Watson and the witch spun into their separate areas and swept through the back rooms of the modest office units.

A faded poster of Nadina, an attractive Light Elf famous for her success on a barbecue reality show and subsequent cooking career, hung on the wall advising children to floss and brush their teeth. Another poster admonished patients to avoid questionable quick-fix magic and rely on proven dental techniques.

Agent Watson rejoined the witch, and they hurried down the hallway to check on the third member of their team. They continued warily, their senses on alert until they reached the cafeteria area, where the third agent pointed his wand inside. His brow was furrowed in obvious confusion.

A quick sprint brought his two teammates alongside.

The lead agent blinked, not sure how to react to what was in front of him. He shook his head as if he could dislodge the odd vision.

Three pairs of human-sized pink teddy bears danced in the mostly empty space, a surprising elegance to their steps.

"What are they doing?" Agent Watson asked.

"I'm fairly sure it's a waltz," the witch responded.

He stared at her. "A waltz? Are you serious?"

She shrugged. "I studied ballroom dancing for several years."

The doors on the opposite side swung open, and another PDA team rushed in, only to stumble to a halt as they also stared slack-jawed at the waltzing teddy bears.

Agent Watson shook his head. "Wait. Are all the offices clear?"

The affirmations came quickly.

He gritted his teeth. "Eris got away. Somehow, she knew we were coming, and she managed to escape." Disgruntled, he slipped his wand into the holster underneath his suit jacket. There was nothing left to do but watch the stupid bears dance.

One of the dancers popped and showered glittering multi-colored confetti along with a cloud of stuffing and fabric. The agents jerked back, their wands at the ready. Watson retrieved his wand once more, ready for an attack.

The remaining bears burst in rapid succession and filled the room with a choking cloud of confetti and polyester. The debris didn't all settle to the ground. Much of it clung together in two clear floating messages.

MAGIC SHOULD BE FREE. BEAUTIFUL CHAOS.

Agent Watson scoffed. Despite all their careful government intelligence and tracking, the fugitive witch had escaped again.

"Let's sweep the area, people," he ordered. "She might have left a clue. Something—anything—that will help us identify where she'll go next."

CHAPTER ONE

R aine set her suitcase on her bed in her dorm room. She smiled at Sara and Evie who had both arrived not long before her. Their suitcases were both open, but they were mostly full.

"Have you seen Christie around?" she asked and glanced around the small room as if the perky English blonde was hiding behind the furniture waiting to pop up and chat about her exciting Christmas vacation.

Sara nodded. "She's running around doing some yearbook stuff and ambushing a bunch of freshmen to ask them what they think about the start of their second semester at the school."

"Perfect." Raine raised her hand with a grin.

They all looked around for a moment with mischievous grins before intoning as a group, "Keep an open mind in the age of magic."

Their silver True Cardinals rings appeared around their fingers. They were symbols of their success last semester with problem-solving and thinking as a group. Raine might have led the charge with her stubborn insistence that there was something to find, but all her friends contributed to solving the mystery.

"I went back and forth as to whether I should tell my Uncle Jerry about it," Raine admitted. "I decided against it. What's the point of a secret society if you tell everyone? It's not like the True Cardinals are doing anything bad. What about you?"

Evie pondered that for a moment before she nodded. "I didn't tell anyone."

"Cameron told some of his pack," Raine confessed. "He told me when he came to visit last week." She sighed. "But I get it. He also swore them to secrecy, and I know they won't tell."

"That explains why William said, 'It got out to a few people but not to worry.'" Evie looked thoughtful. "I wonder if Philip and Adrien told anyone."

Raine shrugged. "The damage is done either way. Everyone else will forget about it by the time we have to help with some True Cardinal tests in the future."

Sara peered at her friend and a grin grew on her face. "You've already thought about it, haven't you—the puzzles and challenges for some students twenty years from now?"

"It gave me something to do to distract me during the break when Cameron wasn't there. A lot of my hometown group were out of town on special holiday vacations. According to one of my friends, she'll be all spun up about college admissions next year, she won't be able to relax, and so they wanted a big last trip as a family."

"College, huh?" the kitsune mumbled. "I should

research art schools, or maybe I should try to get an apprenticeship with someone."

"That's what I'll do," Evie replied. "Aunt Beth knows several potions witches who could use an apprentice."

"Why not study with your family?"

Evie shook her head. "They have and will teach me a lot, but my family's always felt the best way to keep our skills up is to be taught by someone outside the family. There are always different techniques and recipes out there."

"It's too bad I'm not already out in the field," Raine muttered with a sigh.

Sara grabbed a few shirts to hang in her closet. "Why? It's wet outside and a little gross right now."

"No, no." Raine waved a hand. "I mean out in the field as in an FBI agent. I know I don't have to go to college because of Agent Connor's help, but I already feel like I'm ready with all the things that have happened to us here."

Evie chuckled. "Why don't you simply enjoy your last year and a half at school without obsessing over the FBI? It's like you said. They've already agreed to let you in early."

Raine opened her suitcase. "Sure, but that doesn't change the fact there are a lot of bad guys out there, and I can't help stop them if I'm here at school. I looked over most-wanted lists from the FBI and DHS during the break. You'd be surprised by how many magical criminals simply run around and do whatever they want. And depending on bounty hunters to solve it is silly." She had more books stored in her suitcase than clothes.

Sara continued putting her belongings away and shook

her head. "It's not like it's your responsibility to personally catch all the bad guys, you know. Even when you join the FBI, you'll still be a new agent, not the head of their anti-magic team."

"I know, but once I'm in the agency, I can set a good example," she explained. "And that means we'll get more magicals." She smiled at Evie. "Like William."

The girl blushed and looked away. "He wants to be in the FBI, but he's not as..." She sighed. "I don't want to sound mean, but he's not as obsessed as you are."

"Obsessed? I guess I am." Raine waved a hand dismissively. "I am obsessed because of my dad. I'm not talking about solving his murder, but the example he set. Think about it. There are probably FBI agents now who are magicals but hide it." She shook her head in disbelief.

"Why would they hide it?" Sara's forehead wrinkled in confusion.

"Because they had to before, and if they came out now and told the truth, it might get them in trouble—even though the whole restriction was dumb, to begin with." She removed a few books from her suitcase and carried them to her desk. They were all on criminology and history. "I also learned something this week that bothered me. It gave me another reason to want to join the FBI sooner rather than later."

"What is that?" Evie asked.

"Eris, the Witch Queen of Chaos," she declared and imparted a dramatic tone to her words.

"As in the Greek goddess?" Sara asked.

Raine shook her head. "Not exactly, but similar. She took that name when she dedicated her life to chaos."

"I'm confused," Evie complained as she finished her unpacking.

"She's a witch, but she's really into spreading chaos and thinks that magic is too rigid and stuff," she explained. "She's done all kinds of crazy stunts. People have been hurt and killed because of them."

Her friends exchanged looks and both shrugged at the same time.

"She sounds like she needs to be arrested," Sara replied. "But what does she have to do with you?"

Raine tapped her finger against her chest. "Not only me." She gestured around broadly. "Us. This entire school. Eris isn't merely some random criminal. She attended the School of Necessary Magic."

Understanding spread across the other two girls' faces.

"She's like the opposite of Noel Tucker," Evie suggested.

"Exactly." She nodded, satisfaction on her face now that her friends began to understand the importance of the witch. "I'm sure they'll catch her long before I get to Quantico, but I'm frustrated. I wish I could be out there to help capture her and defend our school's honor."

Sara chuckled. "And here, I'm more concerned about becoming an artist."

Raine winced. "It's not like that. I don't think everyone needs to go into law enforcement. We all have our jobs." Her breath caught as she processed what her friend said in its entirety. "So you've decided officially, then?"

"I don't know if it's exactly 'officially.' I wasn't sure before." The kitsune sighed. "At first, I thought maybe my family was so happy that my magic came in, they would be happy about anything. But now they've had enough time for that all to settle in, and they still support me becoming an artist. When I think about that, it makes me happy."

"That's good." Raine smiled encouragement.

Evie cleared her throat. "I had a long talk with my family over break, too, about my future."

"Oh?"

She nodded. "It's been hard, but I think I've settled on being a potions witch. We need more out there who don't try to charge people diamonds every time they do something. It's weird. I know we have thousands of years before magic is as strong on Earth as it as on Oriceran, but a lot of people act like it's still 2015 and magic isn't a thing."

"That's great, Evie," Raine replied enthusiastically.

Everyone but Adrien and Raine had been uncertain about their future on some level when they entered school, but now, the paths before them had crystallized into clear realities. Their time there had allowed them to not only master magic but their own hearts as well.

Raine removed the last few things from her suitcase and the smile lingered on her face. The beginning of her time at the School of Necessary Magic now felt distant. The petty bullying concerns of that first semester barely registered in her mind. Only one or two seniors had been difficult, after all, and a great future awaited them.

It would be a great semester, even if she couldn't help the FBI and PDA capture or eliminate Eris.

CHAPTER TWO

R aine settled in at the dining hall table and smiled at the delicious tagliatelle noodles on the plate in front of her. One thing she would never complain about at the school was the quality of food. Uncle Jerry wasn't a bad cook, but he also wasn't an entire team of dedicated kitchen pixies. It always took a week or two to readjust to not having so many excellent meals whenever she returned to Michigan for vacation.

It was also hard to beat the ever-changing spell-crafted ambiance of the dining hall. That evening, the roof illusion was astronomy-themed, and various stars, planets, and asteroids glided gently above them, along with the occasional comet. Several gorgeous nebulae colored the background. Uncle Jerry's home didn't have a bad roof for a normal house in Grand Rapids, but she didn't feel like an astronaut tumbling through the deepest reaches of space when she ate a meal in his dining room.

For a moment, she considered whether she could change that. A lot had changed and she wasn't the same ignorant girl who didn't understand her own magical potential. While she still had a lot to learn as far as better control over her magic was concerned, modest illusion spells were well within her capability. She simply wasn't sure if she would be as impressed if she were the one who changed the ceiling. Maybe the true secret to enjoying her meal was the presence of all her friends, especially since so many of her hometown group hadn't been around for much of the break, if at all.

The entire FBI Trouble Squad had gathered for their first meal of the semester, and Christie had taken a break from fast-talking at freshmen to join her roommates and her boyfriend Adrien at the table.

Raine glanced across the dining hall. Vianna and Madelyn sat in the corner by themselves and both munched on grilled salmon served on a bed of asparagus. There was a fair number of students present in the room, so she was surprised to see the sisters there. Unusually, they waited until the last minute to dash in for a near-secret meal in an almost deserted dining hall. She hoped that meant they were both more comfortable at the school than they had been since they first arrived.

After a moment of consideration, she decided against going over to talk to them. Her relationship with the sisters was at least stable and non-hostile, which was a marked improvement over most of the previous semester.

Their last conversation had at least established that they no longer believed she was trying to bully Madelyn. Despite that, neither sister seemed particularly eager to become close friends right away. The partial rejection still hurt on one level, but she wanted to be respectful of the sisters' needs even though she might wish their response had been otherwise.

Cameron leaned over to whisper into her ear, "Sometimes you have to accept your wins and losses for what they are."

Raine looked at him. She had long since ceased to be surprised when he was able to read her. That was part of what came with being a good boyfriend, shifter or otherwise.

She smiled and nodded. "You're right," she whispered back. "I'll simply have to give it time. If it happens, it happens, if it doesn't, it doesn't. It's not like I'll be able to be everyone's friend when I'm an FBI agent."

Sara clapped her hands once, oblivious to Raine's concern about the sisters. "Okay, you two, you can flirt later. We need to plan for this semester."

Cameron coughed. "We weren't flirting."

The kitsune winked. "And it's not even been that long since you last saw each other. I know you stayed at her house for a week during the break."

"We weren't flirting," he insisted again.

Philip took a sip of his orange juice before he glanced at his girlfriend. "Plan what, exactly?" he interjected. "We already picked our electives."

"No, not that." Sara sighed and shook her head. "Charlottesville. It feels like all we did last semester was go to movies or dinner in town. There's an entire city to explore, and we didn't explore it. Not really."

"We went to different places for...you know," William muttered. "That should count for something."

They glanced at Christie, but she seemed oblivious to

their coded discussion of the True Cardinals mystery as she focused on her food.

"I mean sight-seeing stuff." Sara sighed. "I can't be the only one who wants to see more of the town. It seems like a shame. We've been to Ruby Falls a few times, but we've barely seen anything in this whole other city nearby."

Raine swallowed a bite of pasta. "I've thought about a few places, but where do you want to go?"

"The Fralin Art Museum to begin with. It's part of the university. They actually have a few cool art displays there."

"That sounds interesting."

Evie smiled. "There are a few places I also wanted to go, starting with Cedar Mountain Orchard." She sighed. "Although now that I think about it, it's too late. I wanted to choose a selection of fresh fruit, but that's more a fall thing. Darn it."

William leaned over to pat her hand. "We can do it next fall, then."

"Is there anything you want to see?" she asked her boyfriend.

The half-Ifrit shrugged. "I don't know. Whatever you guys all want to see is fine by me."

Adrien cleared his throat and nodded. "Same with me. I'm not all that interested in sight-seeing, but I don't have a strong objection to it either."

Christie pursed her lips, a faint look of concern on her face for the briefest of moments before her normal cheer returned and washed it away. "I'm really busy this semester —like super-busy because it's my last semester and I have all the yearbook stuff. I've also seen a lot of stuff in town, but that doesn't mean I don't want to go with you all. I won't be able to go on every trip, but if you're going somewhere, let me know, and I'll tell you if I can go." She took a breath after she'd rattled everything off without pause and glanced at Adrien with a loving smile.

The elf boy's cheeks reddened, but his self-control kept him from turning away.

"Magic Donuts, dudes," Philip declared.

Sara peered at his plate. "What donuts?" She pointed to the half-eaten burger sitting there. "That didn't change shape or anything."

"No, no." Philip shook his head. "No, it's a place in town. They are supposed to make some of the best donuts in the state. We've passed it a few times on the way into town, and I always think, 'I'd like some of those donuts.'" He cleared his throat and avoided looking in Evie's general direction. "I love the pixie food, but whenever they make donuts, there's something slightly off. I don't know. Maybe pixies don't *get* donuts."

Evie harrumphed.

Raine laughed. "I'm sure we can get donuts sometime."

"What about you, Raine?" Philip frowned. "I don't want to go to the library in town. No offense, but if you've seen one library, you've seen them all."

She scoffed. "I don't want to go to the library. At least not together or at first. No, if I want to see anything, I'd like to see the Raven Room."

"Raven Room? What's that?"

"Edgar Allen Poe went to the University of Virginia for one year in 1826. It's his old dorm room. It wasn't until a long time after that people decided to preserve it, but they've brought things in from one of his homes to create atmosphere and authenticity."

Cameron arched an eyebrow. "I didn't realize you were such a fan of Poe."

"I'm not hugely into him, but he basically invented detective fiction with *The Murders in the Rue Morgue*," she explained, and an excited smile crept onto her face. "History plus detective literature together? How could I pass that up?"

The shifter nodded. "It makes sense."

Raine resisted the urge to list a half-dozen other locations she might be interested in—including some of the libraries at the university, despite Philip's complaints. There was one person who hadn't given his opinion yet, and she didn't want to overwhelm his contribution with her own.

"What about you, Cameron?" Raine asked. "Where do you want to go?"

"Maybe some of the hiking trails." He shrugged. "I don't have anything special that I'm dying to see, but sometimes, you want to see different parts of nature and not smell the same kinds of things."

"It sounds like we have plenty of choices this semester and for next year, too," Sara observed.

Raine lifted her head to stare at a passing image of a comet. For all the glories and wonders of magic, there remained enchantments that the regular world could offer. Maybe her friends were right and she needed to enjoy school before she committed the rest of her life to pursue dangerous fugitives all around the country.

CHAPTER THREE

"Are you sure you don't want any coffee, Eleanor?" Xander asked as he stepped into his living room with two mugs in hand. He offered one to Mara who sat beside Eleanor on his couch.

The witch shook her head. "I'm fine but thank you for asking."

He resisted a slight smirk. The fact that she knew to come knocking on his door when looking for Mara proved that no one was deluded about the nature of their relationship. Then again, neither Mara nor Xander had gone out of their way to hide it either. After everything they had both been through, worrying over the appearance of impropriety was fairly low on his list of concerns. It wasn't like they made out in front of the students.

Eleanor cleared her throat after she'd given Xander and Mara time to take a few sips of coffee. "I know we're all very busy with the start of the semester, but I wanted to touch base with both of you to discuss the summer research project proposal I brought up a few weeks ago. We'll need to start on the formal planning."

Mara set her mug down on the coffee table atop a thin quartz coaster. "I think it's a good idea, and this will be a good group of students to pilot-test the program considering we have fewer…external threats than we did a few years ago."

Xander resisted a snort. Interference from ambitious dark wizards lurked constantly as a threat to the school, as his own poisoning a couple of years before proved, but the headmistress was right. Even though the incidents the FBI Trouble Squad had been involved in were dangerous, they also didn't point to a continued conspiracy against the school. The previous semester had been mostly free of any dangerous threats. It was as good a time as any to talk about a summer project.

Eleanor nodded. "I'm glad you agree, Mara. Do you have any thoughts on staffing and numbers?"

"I do," the headmistress replied. "I've already reached out to some of the other North American schools, and I've found a good project for our students. Are you familiar with the Magical Multitudes Project?"

"Whimsical name aside, it's my understanding that it's an ongoing zoological and botanical survey of magical animals and plants in areas without much human presence. In particular, they focus on areas that weren't already exposed to a high level of magical energy prior to the beginning of the opening of the gates."

Mara picked up her mug to take another sip. "That's a good summary. Many different researchers are working on it, both magicals and non-magicals, but it turns out there are two professors at the Orono Academy for Arcane Studies in Maine who have been involved in the project from the beginning. They're taking a small number of students from their school to perform some surveys of a small island off the coast of Maine."

Xander took a seat on the other side of the coffee table. "There are a few islands off the coast of Maine. What's so special about this one?"

Eleanor nodded and her curious gaze returned to Mara.

The headmistress glanced from one professor to the other before she continued. "It was initially off-limits to the general public after the gates began to open. This was because of an unusual level of magical creatures present despite it being nowhere near a kemana or having obvious mineral or crystal deposits that might have absorbed background energy."

Mara tightened her hand around her mug for a moment and gazed past Xander as if stuck in a memory of the past. "They've done some overflights with drones, as there doesn't seem to be any particular interference that makes that level of reconnaissance difficult. But the dense forests and the nature of some of the creatures still require an on-the-ground presence. They're sending two professors and nine students, so I suggest we also send two professors and nine students. It'd be for about two months, so the students would still have a small break before heading to the island."

Eleanor leaned back against the couch. "That seems perfectly reasonable. I presume since it was my idea, I would be one of the professors escorting the students."

"They have some cabins and the like already in place, so it won't exactly be camping."

The professor laughed quietly. "I'm not totally helpless, but I do appreciate something a little more civilized. That's one professor. Who did you have in mind for the second? Lucy?"

Mara sighed. "It's not as if our side needs to provide subject-matter experts, and although I wouldn't do this if I didn't believe the students were safe, I am still concerned about the possibility of trouble. I think someone a little more...seasoned in certain types of trouble might be helpful." Her gaze shifted in Xander's direction.

The corners of his mouth turned up. "I wonder what Agent Oliver would think of sending someone like me off with a bunch of students to some small island, but I don't object. It'd be entertaining to teach in a different environment."

"Agent Oliver might be doing an investigation, but this is still my school," Mara replied. "Besides, you're also an excellent teacher." She turned to Eleanor. "I presume you have no objections?"

The other woman shook her head. "For a moment, I was worried you'd insist I do it on my own."

"Not for such an unusual situation. I've no worries about your ability to handle a small number of students on a trip, but if for any reason something does go wrong, I don't want the government to use it as an excuse against our school and claim we weren't properly prepared. So, if Orono is sending two professors, we need to as well."

"Staffing's the simple part," Xander observed. "Selecting the right students is the more complicated problem."

"I agree," Eleanor stated. "As I suggested during my initial proposal, we need students who have already proven themselves enough to be trusted with general travel, but I suspect most seniors wouldn't be eager to stay another summer. The best choice is to select from amongst the juniors."

"There is good talent in that pool." He picked his mug up and took another sip, far too pleased by how good a cup of coffee he could brew without any touch of magic. "But we could easily create bad feelings if we're not careful with how we select the students."

Mara frowned and stared at the coffee table as she considered this. "I suspect it'll be less of a problem than you might think."

"Oh?"

"You're right about the seniors, and I think it's best for the morale and integrity of the project to keep the choices all from the same grade. If this works out, it will become something that students look forward to. We can hopefully expand the scope of the project in the future, along with the number of students who can participate." She looked up with a slight frown. "Despite that, I imagine that at this point, many students will balk—even as juniors—at spending two months with professors on some small underdeveloped island. Especially when they would likely be under fewer restrictions when at home during the summer. Not only that, given the events of the last few years, many parents might not feel comfortable with the students under school control but in a less warded environment."

Eleanor sighed. "I can see your point, but even if we

assume a flat fifty percent lack of interest, that still leaves a good number of students."

Xander smiled. He had a few ideas about whom he would like to see on the trip. "What you're saying is that it would be great if we had students who had already proven that they could handle themselves in stressful situations outside the school setting without the professors there to hold their hands?"

Eleanor's eyebrows raised. Her expression settled, and a knowing smile appeared instead.

Mara nodded. "That would be a useful combination of traits, and I'm sure we could find at least *some* students who satisfy those criteria. I'm certain, in fact, that we would be able to fill most of those nine slots easily when you put it that way."

His grin split his face. "Then we have the staff, and we have the students."

"They still have to agree."

"If we're all thinking of the same students, there's no way they *wouldn't*."

Eleanor nodded. "Be that as it may, I still think we should get some of the details finalized with the OAAS before we speak to any students."

"Agreed," the headmistress replied.

Xander nodded, his grin still on his face. Taking the students on the ultimate field trip was too much fun to pass up.

CHAPTER FOUR

Raine shifted a little to get comfortable in her seat at her table beside Sara as Professor Powell tapped his wand against his palm. He surveyed the class with a mischievous gleam in his eye. That semester, she was in the same dark magic defense section as Sara, Evie, and William. She was pleased to have a few of her close friends with her—not always a guarantee in every class.

Unfortunately, there were also a few people she didn't care for in class, such as Paige. While Raine had hoped that eventually, the girl would grow friendlier toward her despite their trouble during their freshman year, Paige's attitude had only hardened during their time together at school. In contrast, Madelyn and Vianna might eventually want to be friends, but Paige appeared destined to dislike Raine all the way to some future reunion decades in the future.

"I hope you all had a relaxing vacation," Professor Powell announced and twirled his wand between his fingers. "To the best of my knowledge, none of you had to deal with any trouble that might require the skills of this class during your vacation. But you are students, so for all I know, you fought off a whole horde of murderous beasts during your break and didn't bother to tell anyone."

The class laughed.

Sniffing around for trouble during break didn't sound outrageous to Raine. It wasn't all that different than what she had done with the druids when she'd first arrived at school or any of the other escapades the FBI Trouble Squad had been caught up in. There had to be mysteries in Grand Rapids that needed a good witch's effort to solve.

The professor's gaze settled on her for a moment and the corners of his mouth turned up in a smile. "For our first unit this semester, we'll concentrate on what I like to call tactical creativity. I've discussed this in different ways before. Now, I've simply given it more of a name."

"Tactical creativity?" she echoed.

"That's right." Professor Powell raised his wand in front of his face. "I've talked to you before about how in true life-or-death battles, your ability to use complex spells is limited by the situation. Not every foe will sit there and wait for you to execute a complicated enchantment. So, the more of the quick-castable variety you have available, the better." He pointed with his free hand at William. "What are the keys to a magical battle?"

"Mobility, damage, and defense," the half-Ifrit responded.

The professor smiled. "I'm glad everything I teach students doesn't leave their heads the minute you leave the grounds."

The boy cracked a grin.

"William's right. Mobility enables you to move out of the way of an attack. With damage, or restraint ability, you defeat an opponent before they can hurt you, and defense helps you survive their attacks." He lifted his wand and uttered an incantation.

A translucent image of the professor dodging a fireball appeared. It cycled with an image of him launching a white orb and his shield absorbing a hit from an azure bolt.

Raine, Evie, and Sara scribbled notes as the lecture continued.

"In a sense, mobility is related to defense." The image vanished. "It's about avoiding sustaining the damage yourself so you don't have to move onto testing your magical healing ability, but we've talked about other ways to do that in the past. Can someone tell me one besides restraint?"

Evie stopped writing and raised her hand.

Professor Powell nodded at her.

"Distraction," she stated.

"Good, good. And what are some examples of distraction?"

She looked down for a moment as if considering this. "Sun flare potions to blind an opponent, or kaleidoscope spells to make it hard for them to see."

"Excellent, Evie," Professor Powell declared. "All true. One thing I've found is that people have an inherent bias toward...let's call it flashy magic for effect, when something more straightforward can accomplish the same thing, and that's where we'll begin today." He smiled. "I'll need two volunteers who don't mind too much about getting dirty." He winked. "Don't worry. I'll clean you up after we're done."

Raine's hand shot up first, followed by the hand of a tall, black-haired girl with striking blue eyes.

He nodded and motioned to the front of the room. "Raine and Juniper. Please step forward."

Juniper had experienced some difficulty in driver's ed the previous semester, but she never lacked for courage. Raine didn't talk to her all that much, but they got along well enough. They merely ran with different crowds.

The girls pushed back from their tables and headed to the front of the class.

Professor Powell walked over to his desk at the side of the room to open a drawer. He retrieved two pairs of plastic lab goggles, returned to the girls, and held the eyewear out. They both hesitated before they took them and slipping them over their eyes and nose.

"Take away an opponent's senses, and you're a good way toward defeating them if they're a humanoid," the professor explained. "Take away a humanoid's ability to see, and you cut off about eighty percent of their standard sensory input."

He gestured for the volunteers to stand at the front of the room. They both complied.

"Like Evie said, certain light spells and potions can accomplish that," he continued. "There are also actual blinding spells, but those tend to be very difficult to accomplish in the middle of a fight, especially without physical touch." He raised his wand. "But light spells don't work if someone uses a filter spell, or if they simply don't look. I once resisted a flash spell by doing nothing more than closing my eyes."

Raine was impressed. Sometimes, the simplest solution was the best.

"There's always a more permanent way that's relatively easy to achieve with sufficient training. Ready, girls?"

Juniper swallowed before she and Raine nodded.

Professor Powell looked far too satisfied with himself as he rattled off a quick incantation. A viscous mass of thick green slime winked into existence and splattered over the witches to coat their upper bodies and goggles.

Juniper yelped in surprise. Raine wiped the goo from the front of her goggles. She didn't exactly like being coated in slime, but she didn't want to lose control in front of her friends or the rest of the class. Hopefully, she could get everything out of her hair with normal shampoo—although the professor had said he'd clean them up, whatever that meant.

The entire class's stunned silence lasted for only a few seconds before they erupted in laughter.

Paige giggled in the corner as she watched Raine.

Professor Powell waited for the laughter to die down before he spoke again, but Paige frowned and demanded, "Why is her standing there and getting slimed impressive? Anyone can stand somewhere and be hit by a spell."

"Because her first instinct was to keep calm and restore her vision," Professor Powell explained. "Not to worry about anything else—or even if she'd been hurt—but to restore her vision." He looked thoughtful. "That might be the kind of instinct that only comes from actually experiencing life-or-death situations."

The snarky teenager rolled her eyes but didn't say anything else about Raine. Instead, she fell back on general sarcasm. "Will this really even be useful? Are you seriously telling me that if something like another attack on the school happened, throwing slime around might help?"

Professor Powell raised his wand and ignored the girl for a moment as he cast another spell with a flick of his wand. The slime on Juniper disappeared with a sizzle and vanished into citrus-scented smoke. He repeated the spell for Raine.

She blew out a breath in relief.

"I'm alive today because I once slimed a very disagreeable wizard who was about to—not to put too fine a point on it—blow me up," Professor Powell explained. "So, yes, it can be useful." He pointed his wand toward the door. "We'll go outside to practice. First, we'll go over in detail how to cast the spell, then I have dummies for you to slime. It'll take you a lot of practice before you can complete it quickly, but who knows, maybe someday in the future, slime will save your life." He tossed his wand into the air, clapped his hands once, and snatched it before it fell to the floor. "Let's go."

CHAPTER FIVE

Professor Powell marched the class through the hallways, outdoors, and around the side of the main building until they arrived at a row of dummies made of twisted leaves and grass. Four kitchen pixies hovered over them with anticipation on their tiny faces.

"Thanks for coming," Professor Powell mentioned to the pixies. "I don't know if we'll need you, but this lesson can get messy. I'm sure Horace wouldn't be too happy with me if I spread too much slime around, and we don't want the students to track anything anywhere."

The pixies all giggled and nodded. They flew to the side, well away from the targets.

"I thought we were sliming the dummies," William commented with a small frown of confusion. "Not each other."

"You will slime the dummies," the professor replied, and his grin lingered. "If all goes well, we won't need any help for you. If not...you'll see. First, though, we need to go over the incantation and the technique a few times. You'll use shields, just in case, but note that the spell I'm about to teach you has a slight magic clinging component to it."

"Meaning what?"

"Meaning the slime won't bounce off. It's actually one of the reasons the spell is useful. Basic magical defenses might save a person from getting dirty, but they won't immediately restore their vision."

Raine narrowed her eyes and pointed her wand at her dummy. Most people had trouble even releasing the spell. The incantation was deceptively simple, but the rhythm and tone were actually critical to the successful delivery of the spell. In fact, she had trouble herself.

The students were lined up to face their targets with one dummy between two students.

A small splatter of slime appeared and coated Raine's dummy. It wasn't the kind of dramatic coverage that would save her if she encountered a hostile wizard, but at least it was progress, however small.

She smiled and turned to Evie. Her friend's face was a mask of total concentration as she gripped her wand with both hands, her attention focused on her target. She moved the wand and all but shouted the incantation.

A small amount of green slime appeared but immediately hurtled backward. Evie's shield protected her clothes and face. It was rare that she had more trouble than Raine when it came to magic.

Paige snorted from a couple of rows down. "I haven't even bothered with a shield."

"Maybe that's because you're still not very good at them," Sara retorted. "And you haven't managed to do the spell yet."

The girl rolled her eyes. "Why don't you make some more cupcakes, kitsune? Besides, you heard what Professor Powell said. The spell can cling to shields. Even *if* I make a mistake, I'm safer without a shield than with one."

Raine looked around for Professor Powell. He was a little way off, helping several other students, including Juniper. Slime slid slowly off the girl's shield, and she groaned.

"Show us what you've got then, Paige," Sara challenged.

Paige harrumphed and pointed her wand at her dummy. She shouted her incantation. A massive blob of slime rocketed back and coated her from almost head to toe.

Raine chuckled and waved her wand. "We need some clean-up help here!"

A pixie flew toward them, her arms folded. She clucked her tongue and circled Paige while she moved her hands. The slime sizzled, turned to smoke, and disappeared a little faster each time the pixie completed a circuit.

The girl's face remained tight and annoyed. She pointed at Sara. "It's your fault, kitsune. You messed with my magic."

Sara snorted. "Oh, please. Give me a break."

Raine lowered her wand to aim it at a dummy and enunciated the incantation. More slime coated her target.

Paige marched up to Sara, glaring, but held her wand at her side. "Your friend can cast it without trouble. Isn't that convenient?"

Evie sighed. "I couldn't."

"You sabotaged me!" she yelled.

The students all stopped and looked at the shouting student.

"I didn't sabotage you," Sara replied, her arms folded. "You simply can't do the spell. Don't blame me if you can't pull it off. I never blamed anyone for my magic problems."

Paige's face reddened, and she waved her arms. The few remaining traces of green slime made her look like some angry Oriceran slime monster rather than an intimidating bully.

Raine found the whole thing pathetic. Whatever small power the girl had in their freshman year, she'd long since lost it, but on occasion, she still believed otherwise.

Professor Powell approached her, his face tight. "No one's sabotaged anyone's spells today. Any problems you have are because you don't perform the spell correctly. Given the amount of slime on you, I can even tell that you said the spell too fast and too loudly, and you didn't use the correct angle of the wrist-flick like I emphasized when I was demonstrated." He gestured toward Evie and several other students with slime on their shields. "You're not the only one who has trouble, Paige. What you need to do is simply keep practicing. It's a deceptively simple spell, and again, many people are learning that today. Nothing more. Is that understood?"

Paige's face twitched. She took a deep breath but no

open defiance against the professor followed. She sighed, muttered, and wandered back to her dummy.

Raine looked away to avoid laughing.

The professor gestured to the targets. "Let's get back to sliming those dummies. A lot of them look cleaner than you students do."

CHAPTER SIX

"Sometimes, I wish the movie room had windows," Philip declared as he set out bowls of popcorn and another large box filled with different types of candy, including Whoppers, Milk Duds, Junior Mints, and a small bag containing Hershey's Kisses.

"Windows?" Raine asked. She moved over to the DVD player and opened the case. "Why? A good theater should be dark."

"I don't know. Maybe I want to air it out on occasion."

Cameron sniffed at the air. "It smells fine to me."

Evie and William settled in on a couch next to one another, the half-Ifrit's arm around his girlfriend's shoulders.

"What's our first film of the semester?" William asked. "You never told us what it would be, Raine."

"*Casablanca,*" she replied.

"I've seen that film," Adrien said with a slight look of unease. "It has its...interesting points."

Christie was busy with some yearbook duties, and Raine wondered if that was why Adrien looked unhappy.

William sat there for a moment, his brow furrowed as he processed the title. "Doesn't that simply mean white house? What is it—some sort of foreign thriller about American politics?"

Raine laughed. "No, it's a famous film from over a hundred years ago about the city of that name in Morocco, and I think it's the Portuguese version of the city's name. The film stars Humphrey Bogart and Ingrid Bergman. It came out in 1942. It's kind of romance, but it's also about doing the right thing during wartime. It takes place during World War II with many different factions and groups."

"1942?" Philip laughed. "This film might as well be as old as Librarian Decker."

She rolled her eyes. "We watched *Nosferatu* that one time, and it's older than *Casablanca*."

"But that's horror, not...uh, dramatic romance." Philip shrugged. "Some genres age better than others."

"Hey, I know this one," Sara replied. "Isn't that where he says, 'Play it again, Sam?'"

Raine shook her head. "Actually, that's a common misconception. The main character, Rick, never says that. His ex-girlfriend Ilsa says, 'Play it' to Sam, the piano player, about an old song important to both of them, and later Rick says, 'Play it' too, but he never says 'Play it again, Sam.'"

"Huh. You learn something new every day," the kitsune replied.

Raine grinned. "Like sliming?"

"That, too."

She slid the DVD into the loading tray and pressed the close button. "If we're a movie club, it's important to watch classics. I've thought about how we should watch the top ten films from the last one hundred and fifty years or so of movie history, so we can be true cinephiles."

"Maybe we don't need to go that far back for the top ten," Cameron suggested. "But it's nice to go way back every now and again."

The DVD menu popped up, with "As Time Goes By" as the menu music.

She moved to take a seat beside Cameron. "Let's get started."

Raine ejected the DVD and nodded when she noticed that the others wore thoughtful looks. The old movie had obviously affected them more than she'd anticipated.

"It's a deeper movie than I thought," Philip admitted. "I mean it's definitely *old* in a lot of ways—and not all of them good—but it did make me think, too."

Sara looked curiously at him. "What do you mean?"

"Raine said it was a romance, but it's really more about sacrifice."

"Plenty of romances are about sacrifice." Evie shrugged. "Remember *The Notebook?*"

The wizard made a face. "Sure, I guess. Let's avoid any Nicholas Sparks for a while."

"You're right, though," Sara agreed. "It makes you wonder."

"About what?"

"It makes me wonder what I'd sacrifice for love." Sara sent Philip a playful grin.

The boy swallowed and nervousness spread over his face. "It does?"

"Sure," Cameron interjected. "I mean Rick loved Ilsa, but in the end, he sacrificed any chance of being with her to make sure she was happy and safe. He even put himself at risk of getting executed. It's not like Captain Renault had to mislead everyone about what happened."

Adrien sighed. "I've seen the film twice now, and I'm not sure if I'm disgusted with Captain Renault for being a corrupt Vichy collaborator or impressed that he finally gathered some courage in the end, even if he was forced into it." He shook his head. "I had relatives who fought with the Maquis—the French Resistance—during the war. It's like they've told us in class, magic was supposed to be under control and hidden. At the same time, it's not like the Nazis never used dark magic, so the Guardians couldn't stand by and do nothing, even if certain magical societies weren't sure if they should be involved in such things."

"Renault was more an opportunist than a collaborator," William observed. "He was willing to look the other way for a long time while Rick did all kinds of illegal stuff. From that perspective, he wasn't a true believer in helping the German war machine. I don't know if that makes things better."

A tense silence filled the room.

"You never mentioned this before," Raine said softly to the elf.

"It was a complicated time for my family," Adrien

replied with a shrug. "And a painful one. We obviously aren't unique in that we lost people during the war. But they also say any number of weird magical things happened, too."

Philip nodded. "It's funny, you know? They're supposed to teach us all the hidden history these days, but there's still a lot kept secret. All our lectures on history seem to skip any real details on the kinds of things that really went on during the more recent history. There are still too many secrets out there when it comes to magic."

Raine nodded, pleased that her friends had dug a little deeper. "So all we can do is trust in one another, right? We can find secrets out, whether they're fun like the True Cardinals or dangerous like what happened with Arc Eighty-Eight. It's not like thousands of years of keeping things hidden will all be undone in a few decades." She gestured around the room. "And that's what we're doing at this school, isn't it? Coming together as different kinds of people and learning magic together to push back against all the hidden stuff in the past and the lies that people have spread so we can create a better future for everyone."

A curious look spread across Adrien's face. "That's a good point. There's nothing any of us can do about what happened a hundred years ago, but we can continue to fight against trouble in the future."

Cameron grinned at Raine. "You were really fired up by that movie."

Her cheeks heated. "It's not the movie. But with us almost in our senior year, I've thought more about the future and what it means. I've also thought about how much this place has changed me."

"It's changed all of us, Raine."

Adrien nodded. "I've made more close friends here than I ever thought I would, let alone Christie."

Sara pushed to her feet, her face alive with excitement. Philip immediately looked concerned.

"I know what we should do," Sara declared. "We should all agree right now to five-year reunions after graduation." She held a hand up. "I know what you'll say. 'But, Sara, we'll keep in touch.' Sure, we will, but we'll all be busy, especially William, Raine, and Adrien, given the jobs they plan to do."

"Five-year reunions, huh?" the wizard replied. "I can agree to that. After all, we're all True Cardinals, right?"

Evie smiled. "I'm still not convinced we'll fall out of contact, but I agree."

"Me, too," Raine declared firmly.

Soon, everyone agreed, and a cheerful atmosphere settled over them. No matter what happened in the next few years, they would all see each other again.

CHAPTER SEVEN

The days filled with classes passed easily, along with the initial days of Louper practice. Adrien began to wonder if he'd been hard enough on the team as they approached a crystal-strewn wasteland in their first match. Jagged multi-colored crystal formations, each large enough to dwarf a Kilomea, jutted from the ground, and smaller sharp gemstones protruded from them.

Adrien, Dennis, Hilda, Cody, and Daniel currently played for the Cardinals. Malcolm had been on the starting lineup, but he had hurt his hand in a trap early in the match, so they subbed in Dennis.

The latter freshman now crept forward to take point with a decently layered shield in place as he followed his tracking spell.

"Good job, Dennis," Adrien commented. "Focus on tracking the token, and we'll focus on defense."

"Weren't you the one who said in practice, 'If they allow us to track the coin easily, it means the traps will be nastier?'" Dennis asked.

Cody and Daniel both snickered.

Even Adrien let a grin through, despite his residual worries about maintaining their undefeated season. "We can't win the match without finding the token. It's as simple as that. We're an aggressive team. Our whole strategy is built around that."

They followed the freshman in a roughly triangular formation but took care not to stay too close together. It would be humiliating to all be taken out by a single spell or trap, especially since they were still undefeated in the season.

The density of the crystal outcroppings increased. They'd seen a few flashes of light not all that long before that they assumed were from their opponents, the Montreal Krakens. The other team was still some distance away, though, if that was any indication. Other than a few pixies with long, sharp claws and a few hungry goblins, they hadn't had much trouble.

A few more minutes of travel brought them to a group of crystals that had grown together to form a roof or canopy of sorts. The tracking spell continued to direct the team deeper into the tighter quarters. They could see at a glance that quick, bold maneuvers such as burst spells would be difficult.

An iridescent wall shimmered, highlighted by the touch of light from the sunless sky. The tracking spell brought the Cardinals to the barrier before it failed abruptly.

Adrien frowned and searched for an obvious entrance. He saw nothing that might indicate one, but now that they were closer, it was hard to ignore the huge gemstones embedded near the bottom center. From left to right, he identified emerald, ruby, sapphire, jade, and amber.

There was a single stone of each type, and they all were about the size of his hand.

"It must be something to do with these," he explained and gestured to the gemstones. "Unless someone sees something else?"

The other players shook their heads.

Dennis craned his head upward and pointed. "There's a little space between the crystals and the wall. Someone might be able to get through. Maybe."

The captain shook his head. "That's a good observation, but my instincts tell me this is some sort of puzzle. Five gemstones, five players. We've seen a few like this before—last season, remember?"

They nodded and waited for instruction.

"Everyone, prepare to touch a stone." He walked to the emerald. "Wait for my order." Adrien reached up and waited for the others to position themselves. "Ready. Go." He touched the emerald and it glowed bright green.

Hilda had touched the ruby at the same time. It also lit up—unsurprisingly, in red. The others had also pressed their different gemstones at the same moment, and they all glowed, but their light faded a moment later and nothing of significance happened.

"So…it's not simultaneous, and it doesn't commit you to anything." The elf frowned in concentration. "Cody, Daniel, cover us while we work on it."

The wizards nodded, turned with their wands out, and moved to either side of the group and watched for the Krakens.

Adrien tried touching each stone in turn. They lit up again but immediately went dark after he touched the amber.

Hilda looked irritated. "That was left to right. Maybe right to left?"

He took her suggestion, but the result was the same. His chuckle revealed his chagrin. "I don't know enough chemistry for other suggestions based on their properties, but it won't be that complicated."

Dennis pointed with his wand at the amber. "Alphabetical?"

The captain touched the amber, and a yellow light suffused it. The emerald came next, followed by the jade. He finished with the ruby and finally, the sapphire. The lights didn't dim and instead, they grew brighter.

"Something's happening," he shouted. "Burst back!"

The Cardinals all rocketed back, even the freshmen, even though they weren't great with the spell. Adrien had spoken with Professor Powell about teaching the freshmen the spell, and he hadn't objected, provided that they promised to limit its use to mostly Louper and, as he put it, "certain extraordinary situations."

The gemstones vanished in a massive flash to leave a gem-encrusted door with a smooth diamond handle clearly visible.

Adrien crept forward. He summoned a sword and grasped the handle. "Ready?"

The team nodded, their faces set in determination.

He flung the door open to reveal a vast chamber, sloped on both the near and far sides, with a level soil central area. The golden token glinted in the middle atop a silver tray that rested on the sandy floor. That wasn't the difficulty or the test, though.

Five giant, car-sized scorpions made of amber, ruby, sapphire, jade, and emerald skittered slowly around the silver tray. Their tails and front claws twitched ominously. On the other side of the chamber, a door opened, and the five members of the Krakens—all wizards—stepped through, their wands at the ready.

"Cody, Daniel," Adrien murmured. "I want you to burst over to the opposite sides of the scorpions. You should be able to draw some of the creatures off. Hilda and I will take on the Krakens. We don't have to last against them, only stall them."

"What about me?" Dennis asked.

"Once we have everyone focused on us, you take the token. It's a full-offense play." The elf deactivated his sword. "We'll wait until they make a move before we go. Everyone, get ready."

The others nodded and simply waited.

A tense minute passed as both teams stared each other down. The scorpions continued to meander beneath them and paid no attention to the players.

The five Krakens whipped their wands up. Three pointed at their opponents and the other two at the scorpions.

"Go!" Adrien shouted.

Cody and Daniel's burst spells careened them to either side of the arachnids as the Krakens fired a volley of spell bolts toward the Cardinals and sentries. Adrien and Hilda ducked and rolled down the hill, relying on gravity rather than magic.

The magical attacks missed the players, but they struck the emerald and jade scorpions. The monsters spun toward the Krakens and charged with lightning speed that contrasted greatly with their earlier staid pace. The wizards backpedaled, their eyes wide. They'd clearly miscalculated.

Cody and Daniel launched fireballs at the other creatures from both sides to draw them off.

The elf vaulted to his feet and brought his hands up to cast a quick kaleidoscopic flare spell at the already distracted Krakens. Several of them groaned and stumbled as the two attacking scorpions crested the incline.

Hilda moaned from the bottom of the slope and clutched her ankle. A sprain would be simple enough to take care of after the match, but they didn't have time for a substitution this close to the end.

Adrien burst forward and thrust himself toward the Kraken's side of the chamber. Three of their members, squinting and still half-blinded, supported a joint dome shield that the two monsters clawed and stabbed at with their tails. The attackers hadn't broken through, but the players were trapped and wouldn't go anywhere in a hurry.

The Cardinals captain threw quick light orb spells at the other two opponents, more intent on diverting them than as any real attempt to eliminate them. They backpedaled and took a moment to strengthen their shields rather than counterattack.

Cody and Daniel continued to burst away from the pursuing scorpions and released a few magical blasts every now and then to keep their attention.

Even if it hadn't gone off exactly the way Adrien had

planned, there were no arachnids near the prize. It was all on Dennis, now. He might have been cocky when he joined the team, but he'd slowly improved in both technique and attitude. This was the time to test that.

The freshman charged down the slope as he didn't quite trust his questionable mastery of burst magic. Both the Krakens and the scorpions seemed to realize what was going on at the same time. The creatures immediately lost interest in Cody and Daniel, spun as one, and rushed toward the token.

The elf's efforts and the two remaining scorpions on the other side kept the Kraken players too busy to offer any resistance.

Dennis barreled headlong toward his target and his long strides helped him to close quickly. He thrust forward at the last moment and reached for the gold disc as the amber scorpion brought its stinger-tipped tail back. His fingers snagged the treasure as the monster struck.

The attacker vanished as the freshman slammed chest-first onto the hard-packed earth, the token gripped tightly in his fingers.

The Cardinals remained undefeated.

CHAPTER EIGHT

Mara took a deep breath and shook her head, her hands clutched tightly together on the desk. She didn't want to believe what Agent Oliver had just told her. The PDA agent had been rather quiet that semester. She hadn't conducted any interviews and mostly reviewed school records. Now, the reasons for that were clear. She was obsessing over Eris.

The headmistress remembered the now notorious witch from when she was still merely Lisa. She had always been a quirky girl who chafed under the rules and restrictions of the school. Her fondness for pranks would have made the Live Unnecessary Tricksters blush, but she had never been cavalier or harmed people with her pranks. While it was impossible to teach thousands of students without a single one ever walking down a dark path, that didn't make it hurt any less.

"You're sure?" Mara asked. "She's coming this way?" She glanced at Xander and Bruce, both of whom sat as grim-faced in their chairs as she felt.

Agent Oliver nodded. "We've been lucky to get sightings. Those, combined with a few witness statements, make it clear that she's heading toward Ruby Falls. She even asked someone about good places to eat in town as she said she hadn't been there in years."

The headmistress scoffed. "She wants to take the time for a quick bite to eat between everything else?"

"Whatever you think you know about this witch, forget it. She's not the same girl who attended this school. Her mind is warped. Her goals are warped."

"How can you be so sure she's coming to Ruby Falls?" Bruce asked, his arms folded. "We both know how unpredictable Eris can be. If it were a matter of simply anticipating her movements, she would have been caught a long time ago. For all her talk of chaos, she seems to put a lot of effort into hiding from the authorities. Her mind might be warped, but she'd not mindlessly insane either."

"We're not sure, but it's our best estimate," the woman admitted. "She's erratic, which does make it more complicated. Obviously, she could have portaled into Ruby Falls anytime she wanted to, but she hasn't for some reason— maybe to throw us off as part of a plan, as you suggest. But overall, her movements still take her inthat general direction, even if she sometimes moves away. It's clear from what we've seen over the last few weeks that when she moves in this direction, it always brings her significantly closer to Ruby Falls."

Mara unfolded her hands. "This still sounds like a lot of supposition. If she sometimes changes direction, it might be mere coincidence that she gradually draws closer to

Ruby Falls. Maybe the witnesses misunderstood what she was saying."

"Perhaps." Agent Oliver frowned. "But if that woman shows up, you can't risk any of the students. She's more dangerous—in a fundamental way—than many of the other threats to this campus because of her unpredictability."

Xander chuckled. "But your prediction is that she'll do something specific."

She ground her teeth in evident frustration. "I'm reporting collated intelligence to help protect this school."

Mara sighed and held up a placating hand. "I appreciate what you're doing, Agent Oliver. But based on everything you've told me, she might show up two days from now or two years, and why Ruby Falls? What does she hope to find there?"

"That, we don't know. She might merely think it's a good place to play a few jokes."

Xander sighed and all the mirth faded from his face. "It might not be Ruby Falls at all."

They all looked at him, a little startled.

"What do you mean?" the headmistress asked.

He shrugged. "Lisa—or Eris, or whatever she wants to call herself now—attended this school in the past. It's not impossible that she's coming to the school for some reason rather than Ruby Falls. Someone moving in the general direction of Ruby Falls is also moving in our direction."

Agent Oliver nodded. "I'll admit that is a possibility. But none of the other intelligence we received suggests interest in the school, including the aforementioned witness statements. Although you have your various artifacts stored on the campus, there's more raw power available from the kemana. She might be meeting someone there."

Bruce unfolded his arms. "What's the PDA's plan? I assume you have one."

"Additional agents, for one. Eris might be tricky and powerful, but she's nothing a group of agents can't handle if we can surprise her."

Mara frowned. "I wasn't informed of any additional teams. The impact of multiple PDA agents on campus on the students can't be easily ignored."

The other woman's mouth twitched with what could have been amusement. "They won't be sent to the school. They'll be deployed to Ruby Falls. The PDA has already been in contact with the local authorities to establish an appropriate liaison. As the agency doesn't anticipate that Eris will attempt to breach the school, we see no need reason to station additional agents here. If PDA intelligence suggests otherwise, we can revisit the other question in the future. That notwithstanding, I can assure you, the government has maximum interest in making sure children are not injured. No matter what else you think of me, I hope you understand that."

"Thank you." The headmistresses released a sigh of relief. The last thing she wanted was a large group of twitchy government agents all over the campus to make the students nervous, or even worse, somehow attract Eris to the school.

The PDA agent took a deep breath and adjusted her glasses. "I've spent enough time at the School of Necessary Magic to appreciate the current level of your defenses. I have my quibbles, but it's obvious to me that it would be difficult for a single witch, even Eris, to breach them without you becoming immediately aware. With all the professors here, gnomes, and pixies, in addition to PDA forces deployed close by in the kemana, I'm not all that worried about the school. I only worry about students who might be in the kemana."

"Good. The students shouldn't have to worry about a threat that might never even show up. For now, we still have an education to impart. If new information suggests that Eris is actually in the area, we can withdraw kemana privileges for as long as needed and be stricter about their enforcement."

Agent Oliver nodded. "I'm glad you're being reasonable. If we're fortunate, she'll never come, but I doubt we'll be so lucky."

Xander and Bruce exchanged a glance before they nodded.

CHAPTER NINE

R aine smiled as she headed into the library. The quiet
settled around her as she entered, and the scent of
old books filled the air. She saw the head librarian at the
circulation desk and Joe's back as he disappeared into the
stacks. All the tables and desks were empty.

That didn't bother her. It meant she had more of the
library to herself. Even if she hadn't been able to spend as
much time there that year, it remained a place on campus
that made her happy every time she visited. Her friends
might not have accepted the charms of being surrounded
by so many books, but that was fine. Everyone had their
own likes and dislikes, and she didn't hold it against them.

The mystery of the True Cardinals had been solved by
visiting the library, but Raine wasn't sure if that counted
given how involved Librarian Decker had been in the
whole thing. The principle remained the same, however. A
witch who wanted to expand her knowledge needed to
spend more time at the library.

It also meant she had an escape whenever she needed to

think things over. Although she liked all her roommates and considered them close friends, that didn't change the fact that four girls in one room meant it was almost impossible to enjoy a quiet moment alone in the dorm that didn't involve sleep.

Raine nodded politely to Librarian Decker as she headed toward a corner table in the back to read a criminology book she'd brought with her, along with a copy of a case file provided by Agent Connor. She set her book to the side and opened the folder.

As it was a fraud case, there weren't any gory pictures or anything that would freak out any passing students who saw it. As a true crime junkie and a girl who had known for a long time that she would enter the FBI, she was used to many things that most people, even magicals, still found disturbing. Part of the attraction of joining the agency was to protect people from having to see or experience awful things.

"I've almost found it," a voice murmured behind her.

She turned, confused as to who was talking. She leaned back to glance between a narrow set of stacks near the back. Vianna stood beside Madelyn, an open book in her hand. She pointed to something in the book, a delighted grin on her face.

"Really?" Madelyn asked, her eyes wide with hope.

Raine leaned forward. If they thought she was spying on them, it might cause trouble again. She wasn't trying to eavesdrop. The narrow stacks simply funneled the sound to her. If there were more people present, she might not have even heard, but the library happened to be mostly empty that evening.

"Yes," Vianna replied. "I've gone through some of the books here, and they confirm it. I've also taken a few trips to look for it, and I'm sure I've found it."

"Trips?" Madelyn's breath caught, and she brushed some of her blue hair out of her eyes. "You shouldn't take trips by yourself away from the school. That's dangerous. You told me so yourself."

"Dangerous for you because you let everyone and everything push you around."

"I-I don't want to be like this."

Vianna sighed. "Madelyn, I know. I wish..." She shook her head. "It doesn't matter what I wish. It only matters what I do going forward. All I need to know from you is if you're with me on this. I can't do this by myself. Do you understand that?"

"I know," her sister replied. "But I'm scared."

She scoffed and raised her voice. "We're running out of time anyway." She paused for a moment and lowered her voice. "What did you expect me to do?" she whispered so quietly that Raine could barely make it out. "Just sit around and wait? Do you want to stay at the school or don't you?"

"I-I do," Madelyn stammered. "But I also don't want to lose you."

Raine frowned. She wasn't sure what was going on. From what she'd learned in the kemana last semester, Madelyn had a few strange magical problems related to her being a Coral Elf.

Although everyone often acted like the gates to Oriceran were open and everything was different, the truth was that they were still in the process of opening. As a result, the level of magic on Earth remained far lower than it was on Oriceran. Races that depended on a high level of background magic—such as Coral Elves—who chose to live on Earth could suffer everything from inconveniences to serious problems. Madelyn was a good example as she could, apparently, attract unwanted spirits, among other things.

The only thing Raine couldn't understand was what this all had to do with them staying at the school. The staff now knew about Madelyn's problem, so it wasn't like they intended to kick her out.

Based on what the twins had said, their parents weren't all that supportive. Perhaps whatever Vianna was looking for had something to do with convincing their parents that they should be allowed to stay.

If so, there was little Raine could do about it. She was not all that far beyond where she'd been considered a bully by the sisters. Even if they were on more peaceful ground now, it wasn't like she knew anything about how to convince neglectful Coral Elf parents to allow their kids to stay in a magic school.

The headmistress and the professors must have been in communication with them, and the presence of the sisters at the school confirmed that all hope wasn't lost.

She stood and began to gather her things. Her curiosity made it impossible for her to ignore the conversation, but she didn't want to continue eavesdropping. She purposefully slammed a book shut to warn the sisters.

Joe poked his head out of a stack and eyed her disapprovingly from across the room. She winced and the poppy on his hat emitted a low growl.

"Sorry." She shrugged. "I got excited. I never knew financial fraud had so many interesting aspects."

"Keep it under control, Raine," the gnome replied and shook his head. He popped back into the stacks.

The sisters didn't continue their conversation. A few seconds later, Vianna emerged from the stacks, a slight frown on her face. She carried a book under her arm, but Raine couldn't make out the title.

She offered the elf a smile and a wave. "Hello."

"Hey, Campbell." Vianna nodded into the stacks. "Come on, Madelyn. Let's check out and head back to our room."

Her sister emerged from the stacks, her eyes downcast. She nodded weakly in greeting before she followed her sister toward the circulation desk without a word.

Raine hesitated, unsure if she should leave as well. She'd given the impression that she intended to leave, but her actual reason for departing now walked out the door.

A few curious stray thoughts filtered back into her mind. To the best of her knowledge, the sisters didn't have any roommates. It was unusual at the school for only two students to share a room. Perhaps it was a concession to Madelyn's issues and personality.

Adrien hadn't shared a room with his brother, but they had been in different grades during Etienne's entire time at the school. Christie's presence in Raine, Evie, and Sara's room was a result of trouble with Paige and last-minute rearrangements by the staff.

She sighed and shook her head. A little irritated with herself, she slapped her cheeks to force the thoughts out. Agent Connor had stressed to her repeatedly that keeping an open and analytical mind was a good thing but getting distracted by chasing every half-formed lead could cause an agent to waste a lot of time.

Evidence led the case, but instincts led to evidence.

Raine frowned. What case? She'd solved the case of the Coral Elf sisters already after half-convincing herself they weren't who they appeared to be.

"I obviously can't accept that I was wrong about something and someone didn't like me right away," she murmured.

At least with unpleasant students like Paige, it was easy to not care. On some level, she must have remained disappointed that Madelyn and Vianna had disliked her so severely for so long.

"There's nothing I can do about their parents," she whispered firmly. "The best thing I can do is leave them alone."

That's what she constantly told herself, but there was a small part of her mind that told her there was something more. For the moment, she would have to force it out of her thoughts. She wouldn't cause Madelyn any more pain.

CHAPTER TEN

Bruce stepped into Mara's office. He glanced over his shoulder before he closed the door and took a seat in front of her desk. "You wanted to talk to me?"

"Yes," the headmistress replied, her brow creased with a degree of concern. "As we've had some time to settle into the semester, I wanted to ask you your opinion on Agent Oliver."

He nodded. "First impressions and the truth?"

"Always."

"She's softened up." He frowned. "A lot since the return, actually. I had originally assumed that she didn't interview anyone because I thought she wanted more time to get used to being back here. But we've had weeks, now, and she's done nothing but go through records and ask me a few questions about some of the incidents."

"It might be that she feels interviews are pointless because no one will say anything bad about the school," Mara suggested.

"True, but after the way she came in here last semester,

I don't think that's it. It wouldn't necessarily be hard to find some students who don't like it here."

She chuckled. "Not every student enjoys school, but I would presume that any who dislike it here would complain to their parents anyway. There's not a lot to be gained by complaining to the PDA."

Bruce leaned back and folded his hands. "The other possibility is that she's found a new rabbit to chase—one that has fewer people to help it."

"Eris?"

He nodded. "The PDA wants her badly. I don't think you appreciate how badly. Even if she doesn't have the body count of a terrorist or a high-level magical criminal, she's done something worse to them, in a sense."

"And what's that?" Mara asked.

"She's embarrassed them repeatedly." He chuckled. "For example, they were close to apprehending her a few weeks before the semester started."

"Oh?"

"Yes. Agent Oliver didn't feel free to share that with either you or me. I only found out from some high-level contacts."

"And what happened?" she asked.

"They launched a big raid with a host of agents, only to find waltzing teddy bears and taunting confetti messages." Bruce shrugged.

Mara blinked in surprise. "I see."

"Look, I get it. I've had my frustrations in my time with the bureau. Sometimes, you really want the arrest—the closure. And if that keeps Agent Oliver from accusing half the staff here of being dangerous threats to the students and national security, that's fine with me."

The headmistress frowned. "I'm not sure if it is with me."

"Why?"

She looked at her desk for a moment before she held his gaze. "We have the rest of the semester, but at the end of that time, she'll issue a report. That might very well affect the future of the school."

Bruce scoffed. "I was worried about that for a while but then I realized something important. She's one agent. It's not like she can single-handedly shut this school down, and she's not the only one who sends reports up the chain." He pointed to himself.

"I understand that, but if she issues a negative report, at the minimum, they'll send more investigators—perhaps ones even less inclined to see things our way than Agent Oliver. It'll be difficult to continue without government support." Mara shrugged. "The truth is that we have had a disproportionate number of incidents compared to most other magical schools. I won't deny that, but I will also note that we've taken measures to better secure the campus and protect the students. The parents obviously trust us as they've continued to send students here despite the incidents. While I'm grateful for their trust, that isn't the same thing as satisfying a suspicious PDA agent."

"Setting aside the power of a single agent, I personally think she's started to see things more our way," Bruce replied. "Even before this Eris development, she'd become far less combative and accusatory."

The headmistress shook her head. "I'm not sure that's

the case. The incident, as it were, last semester wasn't a true incident, and she still complained that we allowed the students to be in danger when they investigated Leo and Noel Tucker's secret society."

"Sure, but she could have taken a harder line on that as well."

"I suppose, but how would she react if we had a campus invasion of dark wizards or something of that nature? The kind of incident we dealt with when Alison and Izzie were here." Mara's gaze grew distant and her face pensive.

"I don't know," he admitted. "But all we can do is deal with the incidents we have in front of us now. It's not like nothing has happened. Even if she wasn't on campus, Raine and her friends have been involved in a lot of dangerous things. Agent Oliver is aware of the details of those, and it doesn't seem to have fed her wrath."

She pursed her lips. "We've been fortunate, then, but I'll admit to some slight concern over Eris. If she does something that affects the school, the PDA and Agent Oliver might blame us. I'm confident we can protect the students, but considering the ability she's demonstrated, I can't say it's impossible that she will somehow sneak onto campus. Even when she was a student here and far more stable than she is now, she demonstrated an amazing capacity to avoid the watchful eyes of the staff. She's had years to improve her magic since then."

"Eris? I'm not worried about her."

"Because you don't think she'll come to the school or because you don't think we'll be blamed if she does?"

"Both." Bruce chuckled quietly. "This is where being in

federal law enforcement for decades gives me insight that all your magic can't."

Mara looked amused and raised an eyebrow. "Oh, do tell, Bruce."

"You have to understand the way things work in government law enforcement. The agency that takes point receives most of the glory, but they also take most of the blame when things go south. The PDA wants Eris badly enough that they'll send a group of agents to Ruby Falls based on what amount to rumors, hunches, and desperate guesswork. They've failed to catch her several times, and Agent Oliver is assigned to this school." His expression grew serious. "If, by some bizarre chance, Eris breaks through the defenses—let alone hurts any students here— that's not on you, that's on the PDA for not doing their jobs. They're the ones who have hunted her for years and failed to catch her." He pointed at Mara. "You're a powerful magical, but you're not federal law enforcement. It's not your job to capture Eris. It's your job to teach students."

Relief spread over her face. "Then all we have to do here is maintain the status quo."

He laughed. "Even without a chaos witch, that's difficult enough."

"Isn't it, though?" Mara smiled. "Thanks for your reassurance, Bruce. While I have you here, there's something I wanted to talk about that involves Raine and something we're interested in her doing in the summer."

He leaned forward, his face alight with interest. "Tell me about it."

CHAPTER ELEVEN

The FBI Trouble Squad made their way toward the headmistress's office and all exchanged concerned glances. She had requested that they attend a short meeting in the afternoon, and none of them had any idea why she had done so.

Raine chewed on her lip and tried to think of anything she'd done since the semester had started. "Do you think we're in trouble?"

Evie frowned and William sighed.

Sara laughed. "In trouble? For what? We haven't even done anything we should get in trouble for. We've taken a few kemana trips and visited town a few times. We didn't blow anything up or display any obvious magic. You didn't run off and fight any dark druids or anything."

Cameron frowned. "No one did or saw anything on the museum trip, right? I was with Raine the entire time. Now's the time to 'fess up if you did."

Raine doubted anyone had. If there had been any kind

of trouble at the museum, there would have been more of a reaction when they left.

Everyone shook their heads.

They had taken a quick trip to the Fralin Art Museum on the UVA campus the previous weekend, but they didn't have time to visit the Raven Room.

"They might think we're engaged in other secret society business," Adrien suggested. "And this time, they want us to keep them up to date on what is going on."

"But the staff were in on it last time—or at least one of them was, dude," Philip replied. He shrugged, an exasperated look on their face. "We're innocent."

"We might not be in trouble," Raine replied. "I merely wondered, is all."

"You have me all paranoid. Thanks, Raine," the wizard retorted.

Sara elbowed him, and he shrugged.

They arrived at the office and Raine knocked lightly on the door.

"Come in," the headmistress called.

Raine opened the door and waited for all her friends to file in before she entered and closed it. If they were there to be chewed out, she would prefer that no one else hear it.

Headmistress Berens sat behind her desk, a bright smile on her face. She didn't look like the kind of woman who was about to rip into them for breaking school rules or violating any of their travel restrictions.

"I'm glad you could all join me," she said. "Before I begin, do you have any idea why I've called you in today?"

They shook their heads and made an effort not to look at one another.

The headmistress leaned back and surveyed the students with an appraising eye. "Professor Hudson came up with an idea recently—something she's thought about for a while, but for which the time wasn't right."

Raine nodded slowly. Several of her friends exhaled loud sighs of relief as everyone now fully grasped that they weren't in trouble.

"What's this idea?" she asked.

"A summer field research project," Headmistress Berens explained.

She gasped in surprise. "Really?"

A few of the others exchanged glances. William looked uncertain, but Evie and Adrien both looked eager.

"Yes. As you might have guessed from things like Professor Powell's class, one of our goals here isn't simply to educate you about possibilities, but also to provide you with practical experience in the use of magical abilities. A field research project would be one way to do that, but there are some complexities involved."

The students nodded and waited for her to continue.

"For one thing, parents allow us a large degree of latitude here because of the heavy defenses of the school. Removing students and placing them in a field environment—in this case, a magical zoological and botanical survey on a small and otherwise uninhabited island off the coast of Maine—means less control. Accordingly, our first choice would be students who have already demonstrated self-reliance and a naturally inquisitive nature." She gestured to include all of them with a sweep of her hand. "Such as you seven. There will be nine students selected in total for the project, which will be conducted in concert with the Orono Academy for Arcane Studies."

William smirked. "I hope they aren't too sore over how badly we've beaten them in Louper these last couple of seasons."

Evie sighed and shook her head. Adrien cracked a smile.

Headmistress Berens chuckled quietly. "I'm sure they can put aside our sports rivalry, but before that, we need to discuss this a little more. This is strictly a volunteer activity. I want to make that clear."

"I'm in," Raine said.

Sara nodded. "Me, too."

"How could I not want to go on a magical botanical survey?" Evie asked.

Cameron, William, Philip, and Adrien all nodded.

The headmistress looked surprised. "I must admit, I thought I'd have more difficulty convincing you to do the project. To be clear, this will involve you being on a small island for two months with Professor Powell and Professor Hudson. You'd have a little time off after the end of the semester before the project started. Of course, there are some cabins built there, so it's not like you'll sleep in a tent, but it won't be the accommodations you're used to either at the school or at home."

Cameron chuckled. "I spend a lot of time during the summer in wolf form. I can survive roughing it for a while."

Philip rubbed the back of his neck and grinned. "I think I prefer the idea of cabins rather than having to sleep in the woods. Even with magic, it'd get annoying."

She nodded. "I'm pleased that you're all so enthusiastic. I should also make it clear that other than the two professors from our school and the two professors from OAAS, there will be no other adults accompanying you on this trip." Her gaze shifted toward Raine. "I've already spoken to Agent Connor about this, and he's assured me that he and your guardian don't have any objections."

"I don't need an FBI babysitter all the time." She grinned.

"Good to know."

Adrien cleared his throat. "You said there will be nine students from our school?"

"Yes." The headmistress smiled. "At least on this trip. If it goes well, we'll consider a larger number of students in the future."

"There are seven of us, so who will the other two be?"

"We haven't made a final decision yet, but I can assure you that we want this to be a positive experience. We don't feel this summer project is a time to test your interpersonal skills under difficult environments and conditions."

William frowned. "Meaning what exactly?"

Raine managed not to laugh. "That's professorese for she won't send us with people we don't get along with."

Headmistress Berens smiled. "Let's say we'll make our selection for maximum compatibility."

"Is Christie considered for the project?" Adrien asked.

Raine looked at him. He wasn't as open about his feelings toward his new girlfriend as William, Philip, and Cameron had been, but she knew Christie had spent time in Paris over the winter break. She'd off-handedly mentioned being shown all that was beautiful in France.

The headmistress sighed. "Although she's a lovely girl with many wonderful qualities, we don't feel she's suited for this particular project. In addition, we're trying to keep it all juniors, as we anticipate this will be a post-junior year project. I'm sorry."

Adrien shook his head. "I understand, Headmistress. I was merely curious."

Raine felt bad for him. The rest of them would have their significant others and spend the summer together, but he would be separated from his new girlfriend for two months.

Headmistress Berens steepled her fingers. "To be honest, there are a number of possible choices, but they don't represent the easy, natural fit for the project that you seven do. I should also make it clear that we don't anticipate any trouble. This will be a low-key magical survey. Yes, you will use spells, but we don't anticipate you having to fight anything. That said, there are wild magical creatures on the island, so your experience in defending yourself isn't useless either."

"I'll be eaten by a giant magical bear," Evie joked.

The students laughed.

"The professors should keep that from happening." The headmistress smiled. "Although we don't want you to come to any harm, we'd also like to not disturb the balance too much on the island. We have no idea how rare some of the species there may or may not be, but don't worry too much about the finer details. The professors will help with that when the project starts, but for now, I'm glad to hear you're all eager to participate. We'll contact your parents and guardians individually to secure their permission, but until then, don't worry about it. There's no special pre-training required. That will all be handled on the island this summer. For now, enjoy the rest of the semester."

CHAPTER TWELVE

Cameron looked around the table. William, Philip, and Adrien all sat there with worried expressions on their faces.

They had gathered in the movie room at Cameron's suggestion, even though it wasn't movie night. It was one of the few places where they could have a decent discussion as a group without the girls around. Also, not being in their dorm room meant less chance that someone would track them down to chat.

Sometimes, men needed to discuss a few things between themselves without their women around—at least, that was how Philip had pitched the idea to Cameron. It all sounded rather logical at the time, even though the shifter had allowed creeping doubts to seep in about the whole thing. But it wasn't like Raine would find out. At least he hoped she wouldn't.

Cameron didn't like secrets. A shifter didn't keep secrets from their pack.

The wizard looked over his shoulder, a nervous expression on his face. "They'll find us in here. I know I'm the one who said we should all talk, but maybe we should have done this in the woods or something."

William shook his head. "The woods? I don't want to have some secret discussion in the middle of the woods. Who knows who might be out there? It's not like Dorvu's good at keeping secrets either."

Adrien shrugged. "I'm still dubious about this meeting, but why would the girls find us here? We almost never have movie *day*, only movie night. They have no reason to search for us here, and no one knows we planned to come here."

Cameron grinned. "Exactly." He spread his hands. "Okay, guys, we need to discuss Valentine's Day. Even though Philip is the one who approached me, I figured we should all talk, because he has some points I hadn't thought about before."

"What about Valentine's Day?" William asked. "You said we needed to have a secret meeting about it without the girls around, but you weren't clear on why."

"It's one of the most dangerous days of the year."

Philip nodded in agreement at Cameron's statement, which made sense given that he was the one who had introduced that concept to the shifter.

Adrien scoffed. "What's so dangerous about it? It's not as if the Veil thins on Valentine's Day like it does on Halloween. There are no dangerous love spirits who travel around and try to snatch people to different dimensions."

"Says the elf who is in his first real relationship," Philip mumbled.

The elf in question shrugged. "My personal experience

doesn't change the validity of my question. Why is it dangerous?"

"If anything, Valentine's Day is more dangerous than Halloween. At least you know what sinister spirits might try to do. Girls, though? They're the real mysterious entity. Knowing a little magic won't save you." Philip clucked his tongue a few times.

"It's stressful," Cameron explained and rolled his eyes. "If we screw up our Valentine's Day plans, our girls will be mad at us, and the next few weeks will be hell."

Adrien frowned. "I'm surprised to hear you say that. Raine doesn't strike me as the kind of girl who will harbor a grudge over something so petty. I know Christie isn't." He shrugged, disinterest on his face.

"Sure." The shifter frowned. "But it could happen. You never know." He looked at Philip with slight pleading in his eyes. He didn't want to be the one to have to explain all this. It wasn't even his idea, and he wasn't entirely comfortable with it.

Philip grinned. "Sure, everything's going great until you screw up or something, and then *boom*. You're in the dog house." He winced. "Sorry, Cameron. Poor choice of words. No offense."

"None taken."

The wizard sighed and shook his head. "A few days ago, I had an epiphany, and this will help us all." He spread his hands and his eyes widened.

William eyed him with even more suspicion and confusion on his face than before. "You had an epiphany about Valentine's Day?"

"Yep. It's like business. They invented joint-stock

companies to distribute risk, and I thought we could do something like that. We should work smarter, not harder. That's what we do in the Entrepreneurs Club, and that's what all of us should do when it comes to romance."

"Start a company?" William shook his head, clear confusion written all over his face. "What does that have to do with Valentine's Day? Are we supposed to start a flower company or something? Candy company?"

"No, no, no." Philip waved his arms in front of his face. "I'm talking about the principle of distributing risk." His grin grew even wider. It was amazing that his head could stay together at this point. "That's the key here—the risk. Romance is a lot like business. Don't you think?"

"Uh, not really."

"And how do we go about distributing romantic risk?" Adrien inquired with a raised eyebrow. "I won't claim to be an expert on romance, but I have a hard time thinking that romance is a lot like business. Maybe it's only me being a stiff elf still in need of a Manic Pixie Dream Witch."

"It's simple. We distribute romantic risk with a group activity," the wizard explained. "Probably in Charlottesville. That way, it's not like any of our girls can get individually mad, and if we pool our ideas, we can find an activity they'll all love."

Adrien nodded slowly but his expression suggested he was unconvinced. "I see. Like bowling?"

Philip burst out laughing. "You're joking, right? You want to take Christie bowling on Valentine's Day?"

The elf smirked. "This whole thing seems a little ridiculous. I couldn't resist poking at it."

"You got me, dude. You got me."

Cameron grunted. "Maybe we should all go to the same nice restaurant as a group. That way, everyone has the same expectations, and no one will feel like they were short-changed."

William nodded quickly. "That sounds good."

"No," Adrien declared, and a stern command echoed behind his words. He folded his arms and frowned.

"No?" Philip blinked. "What's wrong with taking our girls to a nice restaurant? You like food. Christie likes food. We're merely talking food with a little more atmosphere. It's not like you can take Christie to a swordfight."

"Yes, I like food." The elf nodded. "More specifically, one doesn't need to have extensive dating history to high-light the major flaw in this plan. Yes, we often do go out together as a group, or even spend a lot of time together in a group during some of the dances. But Valentine's Day is one of the few days that is supposed to be dedicated to couples." He shrugged. "I think it'd be an insult to Christie if I tried to turn it into a group date, and I won't do that to her. I refuse to do that to her."

Cameron frowned. He'd thought something similar, but Philip's pitch had been very convincing. There had been a lot of charts involved. "Do you really think so?"

Philip sighed. "Come on, guys. Distributed risk."

Adrien pointed at the wizard. "Isn't this more about protecting you?"

"Meaning what?"

The elf shrugged. "Raine and Evie have unusually even temperaments. Christie is an overtly positive person to the point that I'm still surprised she's dating me. Sara is loyal and brave, but she also has a more fiery soul than any of the others. As your friend, I understand your concern, but I also, as your friend, would be wrong to not tell you that you shouldn't hide behind us. If I've learned anything since dating Christie, I've learned that much. Sorry, Philip."

Cameron frowned at the wizard and wondered if he was simply afraid of displeasing Sara.

Philip slumped in his seat. "Yeah, maybe you're right. I make fun of you, Adrien, but my relationship with Sara's still new, too. This will be my first Valentine's Day with her. I think that on some level, I'm afraid I'll screw it up and she'll dump me."

"Courage aids in battle, as it does in romance," Adrien declared with a sage nod. He gripped Philip's shoulder and gave it a slight squeeze. "You'll do fine. Sara's not some random girl you barely know. You've known each other for years. She likes you. Don't worry so much. Believe in yourself."

Cameron gave the elf an appreciative look. "You're really not worried about your first Valentine's Day with Christie?"

Adrien shook his head. "As far as I'm concerned, the hardest part is over. I know there will be trouble. I know there will be fights, but nothing worth doing comes easy. If I can fight for my life against the Raven Clan, I can put a little effort in for my girlfriend."

"Dude," Philip muttered. "You went from the guy who could barely understand that Christie was into him to the guy who is now some master of romance. How did that happen?"

"I approach my relationship the same way I approach

everything else in my life—with dedication, honor, and humility. That's what it means to be a Guardian."

"Fine, then it sounds like the group date is off," Cameron said with a smile.

William sighed. "And I was just getting used to the idea."

Philip snapped his fingers. "We don't have to waste a good meeting. Even if we don't do a joint outing, we can still discuss what we all think about individually. That way, we won't make any of the rest of look bad." He looked at Adrien for approval.

The elf nodded. "I think that's a great idea."

CHAPTER THIRTEEN

Raine leaned toward Evie. They were the only members of the FBI Trouble Squad in the same potions section that semester, so it was easy to figure out where to sit. Both of them liked the class and preferred to sit in the front row. Their early arrival led to little competition for seating, but now, the entire class was filled.

Their cauldrons were already set up, and various herbs lay on a tray beside the equipment. Vials filled with different colored liquids rested in a rack sat beside the trays.

"Has William been weird lately?" Raine whispered to Evie. "I'm curious, that's all."

Professor Fowler puttered around the front of the class and adjusted the position of some of her ingredients. A chartreuse potion in a clear flask sat on the table in front, along with a large cauldron that she'd enchanted so the students could see the contents. The class hadn't officially started yet, and the professor often spent a few minutes in preparation before she started instruction.

"Weird?" Evie whispered back. "What do you mean? I don't think so."

"Cameron's acted kind of weird and nervous," Raine said. "I wonder if it has to do with Valentine's Day. It's not like it's a big deal, though. At least, it hasn't been in the past, so I don't know why it would suddenly be a problem this year."

Evie shrugged. "I don't know what to say. William's not been weirder than normal. Not that he's weird—he's just William. If anything, he's quiet."

"Maybe I see something that isn't there." She nodded and her gaze swept over the ingredients. "Too much FBI agent, not enough girlfriend."

"It's okay." Her friend smiled. "It's not like Cameron would ever disappoint you. He's one dedicated wolf."

Raine's cheeks heated, and she nodded.

Professor Fowler set a small soil-filled maroon planter on the table. The first sprouts of a plant had already broken through the surface. She clapped. "Okay, class, it's time to get started. We have an interesting potion unit coming up. Of course, they're all interesting, but this one is even more intriguing."

Raine turned away from her friend to focus on the professor. She might not have Evie's affinity for potion making, but she understood how useful they could be. Professor Powell continually stressed how they needed to be ready with tactics that worked in dangerous situations. One way to be ready would be to carry potions.

There was also the possibility that some potions might be useful for investigation work. Unfortunately, everything she had studied about the law reinforced that the ability of law enforcement to use potions during their investigations was still limited. At least in terms of investigations, anyway, but she would be allowed to use magic if it led to evidence she could have otherwise found. Anything she could absorb about useful spells or potions that might help her with her future career was welcome.

The professor nodded toward her cauldron. "Today, we'll begin work on a potion that can aid with the rapid growth of plants. This is more an exploration of technique, in some ways, because there are many drawbacks to using this particular kind of potion. However, it will help familiarize you with several new and useful ingredients."

Evie raised her hand.

"Yes, Evie?"

"What sort of drawbacks?"

The Light Elf professor picked the planter up with both hands and held it in front of her. "The potion is a true rapid-growth potion, but the plants that grow from it lack most of the nutrition of naturally grown plants. Effectively, you'll get the nutrition you would from a single seed rather than a whole plant. So, this isn't a method to solve hunger."

Evie frowned and scribbled the relevant notes before she sighed. No one was more disappointed when a potion couldn't do everything and anything than she was.

"That's not the only limitation." Professor Fowler set the planter back on the table. "The ingredients for the potion are rather complicated and can be difficult to find, especially the powdered unicorn horn."

Several students gasped and Raine winced. One boy in the corner glared at the professor. Evie sighed and shook her head.

The professor held her hands up. "Don't worry. It's not actually unicorn horn. They call it that because in the distant past, the ingredient—which is actually made from certain rocks exposed to different types of magic—was ground up and passed off as unicorn horn by unscrupulous herbalists."

Raine raised her hand.

"Yes, Raine?"

"If it's actually useful, why lie about it being unicorn horn?"

"Because actual unicorn horn is a rarer, black-market item and, as such, is extremely lucrative to those with poor morals who might wish to engage in unicorn poaching."

Raine frowned, scribbled that information, and underlined it. That kind of anti-magical animal poaching investigation wasn't likely to be something she would be involved in, but it wouldn't hurt to ask Agent Connor a few questions about the FBI's jurisdiction in such cases.

Professor Fowler picked up the chartreuse potion flask and held it up for the class to see. "This is the final color you want. If the potion isn't this exact color, you've failed. I'll hand out the recipe in a moment, but I do want to warn you that following the recipe is even more vitally important than under normal circumstances. There are certain steps that are beyond the scope of classroom sessions—such as bathing some of the herbs in the light of the moon—but I've already prepared everything necessary in such cases." A stern look crossed her face. "That said, be aware that the difficulty preparing some of these ingredients means there is very little to waste. Even with the portioning that I've already implemented, it's important that you make as few mistakes as possible. That's one of the reasons why this potion, although not extraordinarily difficult on a technical level, isn't typically taught until junior year."

The students watched intently, their attention still fixed on the potion in her hand.

She shook the potion a little. "That helps it when it's been sitting for a while."

Her face a mask of utter concentration, she leaned over the planter and tipped the flask slowly toward the sprout to inch the top down. A small drop of the liquid dribbled out and fell on the sprout.

The professor stepped back and righted the vessel. The potion seeped into the plant over the course of several seconds. It would have been hard for Raine to see if she hadn't sat in the front row.

Professor Fowler set the potion down and nodded at the plant. A few seconds later, the sprout grew several inches and thickened as new shoots appeared. Weeks of growth had occurred in mere seconds. A few students responded with oohs and ahs, impressed by the modest magic. Cynicism hadn't eaten their hearts yet.

"Despite the lack of usefulness when it comes to edible plants," the professor continued, "I hope you can see some of the potential for more aesthetic gardening. One might not want to have to replant one's entire hedge maze, as one example."

Evie pointed toward the flask. "You have an entire potion there, but you barely used a drop."

Professor Fowler nodded. "Yes. A drop is sufficient. Too

much doesn't result in rapid growth. It merely results in...
Well, let me show you."

She raised the flask and poured a stream of the liquid
on the plant. Again, the potion seeped into it. This time,
however, it shriveled and died.

"It'll take a long time for you to learn proper dosages,
but a few minor mistakes shouldn't kill your plants."
Professor Fowler tapped the side of the flask. "For the next
week, as we concentrate on appropriate brewing and
dosing, I've tried to limit the difficulty by giving you a
recipe that will produce only a small amount." She frowned
and took a moment to refocus. "Now, after I hand the
recipe out, I'll have you study it for several minutes before
we begin. In that time, I'll distribute some of the last few
remaining ingredients—particularly those that had to be
kept in the dark or cold—and we'll try to brew our first
rapid plant growth potion. This is definitely one where
you'd need a lot of prep time and not as much brewing
time." She headed toward her desk.

Raine wrote all the professor's comments in an
abridged form before she underlined **PREP TIME** with
three separate thick lines.

She looked at Evie with a smile. "Maybe I'll take up
gardening after this."

Her friend shook her head. "I haven't made one of these
before, but I've heard about them. I should have recognized
the ingredients. These are hard to accomplish."

"Well, we have to start somewhere."

Raine glared at her magenta potion as if her baleful attention would spontaneously change the color into the desired chartreuse. The stubborn potion remained its original color.

She sighed. "I thought I followed the directions exactly."

Evie carefully poured a dark-blue herb aqueous extract into her bubbling cauldron. The liquid inside was already the correct color. The dark-blue liquid swirled in the mixture for a few seconds before it disappeared.

"Yours is perfect," Raine said. "That's not a big surprise, but do you have any tips?"

Evie blinked a few times and looked at her. She'd been so focused on her own potion-making, she'd barely looked at her friend for the last few minutes.

"You added too much acorn powder." She pointed to the cauldron. "That's why it's that color. It might still work, but it'll take a lot more."

"Is there any way I can fix it?"

Evie made a face as she gave it some thought. "Use a little more unicorn horn."

"It's not from real unicorns, remember?"

"I know. I've used it before, but I wish they wouldn't call it that."

A petite brown-haired witch yelped in the back of the classroom. Everyone stopped what they were doing to look at her.

Huge green shoots grew from her plant and curled around her arms. Cracked planter shards lay in the spilled soil on her work surface. The roots of the plant continued to grow and twitched as if they tried to dig into the table.

Other students around her backed away and some retrieved their wands.

The girl shrieked. "Professor Fowler, my plant's trying to eat me!"

The professor sighed and marched toward the plant as she clucked her tongue. She raised her hand and uttered a quick incantation. A purple light bathed the still-growing plant, and it stopped its relentless burgeoning.

The young witch pulled her arms gingerly free of the curled shoots and snapped them off the plant in the process.

Professor Fowler rubbed her chin and studied the overgrown specimen. "That's actually impressive, Georgina. Excessive use of the potion should have killed the plant, not made it grow so large without flowering." She nodded. "A fortunate confluence of ingredients and technique. It's difficult to pull off, I can assure you."

"Fortunate?" Georgina squeaked. "It tried to eat me!"

"Of course it didn't try to eat you." She smiled as the plant collapsed. "This is a rapid-growth potion, nothing more. Maybe if you'd done it to a carnivorous plant, it might have tried to eat you, but I don't use those in this demonstration." She frowned and seemed distracted for a moment. "Not anymore, at least."

Raine gasped. "This would be a great non-lethal restraint potion." Her mind ran with the possibilities of how the FBI could capture criminals with rapid-grow plant potions.

Professor Fowler cast another quick spell and Georgina's plant began to shrink, although it didn't look particularly healthy. "That isn't what I'd think to do with it, but I suppose that's true. Maybe that's something you can research in the future, Raine."

"Darn," another student, Malcolm, shouted from the front of the room.

Everyone turned, expecting more plant grappling. His plant was nothing more than a shriveled sprout.

Malcolm shrugged, an abashed look on his face. "I added a good dollop in the hope that it'd grow super-big, too."

The class laughed.

CHAPTER FOURTEEN

Raine smiled as Cameron pulled her chair out for her. She wouldn't have chosen the fancy French place for their Valentine's Day dinner, but there was something about all things French and romance.

It helped that he had been so attentive over the last few days, including accompanying her on a trip to the Jefferson-Madison Library. He looked so handsome in his khakis, crisp white button-up shirt, and dark-blue tie.

She sat and he moved to the opposite side of the table.

"I've never eaten here," Cameron said, "but it has good reviews online."

"When and where did you find the time to go through online reviews?" Raine leaned forward to whisper. "What about all the wards on the school grounds? Even Agent Connor has to get printouts for me because of them."

He grinned and shook his head. "I didn't check it from school. What do you think I did when you looked through all those books at the library?"

"Oh." She blinked in real surprise.

They both quieted as the waitress approached with the menus. She handed them out and took their drinks order, nothing more than water for them both.

"We'll need a few minutes," Cameron said.

"Of course." The woman gave him a bright smile and departed.

Raine opened her menu and scanned the choices for a few moments. "Do you have any idea what you want?"

"Filet de Bœuf. I wanted to order filet mignon, but I read online that in fancy French places if you order filet mignon, that's usually pork or veal." He shrugged. "Somehow, I didn't pick up on that the last few times I've been to a place like this, but I wasn't the one who actually ordered."

"I thought maybe this French Onion soup. It's a French restaurant, after all, so it has to be good."

"You'd think." He chuckled and adjusted his collar.

Raine glanced from the menu to her boyfriend. Secrets could grow into something worse if untended, and they didn't even need a rapid-growth potion.

"What's wrong?" she asked softly. "If you're not telling me something because you think you need to protect me, don't. It's not that I don't appreciate it, but I would think that by now, you know I want a partner, not a protector."

Cameron grimaced. "It's not that. Nothing like that at all, actually. Well…kind of."

The waitress appeared again to rescue him from his discomfort, but Raine wouldn't let him escape her interrogation.

Once the woman took their meal orders and departed, Raine leaned forward. "I'm happy with where you brought me if that's what you're worried about. And flowers from you mean a lot more than they would from most of the boys at the school because you can't use magic to help you find or change them."

He shook his head. "The future."

Her forehead scrunched in confusion. "The future? What about it?"

"I shouldn't talk about this now. Not today. I'm sorry, Raine. You're too good at reading me."

Raine reached across the table to take his hand in hers. "Don't hold it all in, Cameron. Like I said, I know you always try to protect me, but sometimes, let me protect you."

Cameron scoffed. "If only that was it." His eyes flashed yellow for a moment. "We both know what you'll do in the future. You'll join the FBI."

She nodded. "Yes. What about it? You've never had a problem with it before."

"And I still don't. Your fierce focus is one of the things I like about you."

Her cheeks heated, and she averted her gaze. "Valentine's Day is the perfect day for flattery."

"I want to make sure I don't hold you back," he said softly.

Raine stared at her boyfriend, but he wouldn't make eye contact. That was rare.

"What do you mean?" she asked.

"I won't join the FBI. I'm not even sure about the future, honestly, not as much as you are. My ideas about what I want to do constantly change."

She smiled softly in understanding and squeezed his hand in an attempt to comfort him. Knowing

Cameron, he had held these concerns in for a long time.

His laugh sounded a little bitter, and he pulled his hand away. "And now I'm complaining on Valentine's Day. Great boyfriend."

"I won't leave you behind because I join the FBI if that's what you're worried about. We can have a long-distance relationship." Raine laughed. "Things will be different once we're out of school. The internet, phones, spells—I think being at the school warps our view of things." She shrugged. "They let us visit places, but we spend most of our time in a place that isn't like the outside world. Not only that, it's a place cut off from the outside world on purpose."

Cameron straightened, the careful consideration obvious on his face. "That's true."

"Of course it's true. Think about how much we talk during the break. We're not close when I'm in Grand Rapids, and you're at home for most of the break, but it's not like it's a problem."

The shifter cleared his throat. "One thing I want to do is give you the option."

"Option?"

"If you think you'll be held back by me, even though I love you, I understand. Your whole life has led toward you joining the FBI. I want to make sure I don't do anything to stand in the way of your goal, even if that means I have to step aside. I care about you too much." He managed a grin. "It's like Rick said in *Casablanca.* If you don't go into the FBI, you'll regret it—maybe not today, maybe not tomorrow, but soon and for the rest of your life."

"No. I'm changing the script." Raine gave him her best stubborn face. "With a better ending."

"Changing the script?"

"In this script, Rick and Ilsa met each other in school, and they were never separated. Neither of them has to sacrifice anything. They can be together."

"That leads to a short movie," he joked with a shrug. "The ending doesn't have as much punch. No Nicholas Sparks either?"

She scoffed. "No. In the *Notebook II*, they meet and fall in love and grow old together. Allie joins the FBI, and Noah goes into some other wonderful career worthy of him."

"You're sure, then?" he asked, and his normal confidence returned to his voice.

Raine blinked a few times and tears pricked at the corners of her eyes. "I love you, too, Cameron, and no, I don't want you to go anywhere. If we have to spend a lot of time on the phone or a computer between visits for a while, I'm fine with that."

"Oh, man, I made you cry on Valentine's Day. I'm the worst boyfriend in the world."

"No, you're the best boyfriend in the world, and I can't imagine spending Valentine's Day with anyone else."

CHAPTER FIFTEEN

A week later, Raine was in the back of the library reading a new book, *A Revisionist History of the Silver Griffins: A Critical Examination of Pre-Twenty-First Century Magical Control*. So far, the semester had shaped up to be one of her best at the School of Necessary Magic. Her classes had come along well, she was still on a high from her Valentine's Day dinner with Cameron, and her excitement for the summer research project built slowly. The Cardinals remained undefeated, too, and no strange conspiracies or corrupted magicals had tried to draw her into trouble.

A flash of blue caught her attention, and she looked up. Madelyn settled in at a nearby table, her flower backpack already on top.

There was one thing that prevented the semester from being perfect. She wondered if it was time to push forward on becoming the girl's friend. Given the conversation she'd overheard before, it sounded like she could use another person to talk to. Vianna was loyal and Raine could respect that, but she had also learned how important having a lot of friends could be when you needed emotional support.

She took a deep breath and decided that she needed to not come on too strong. No, she needed to not come on strongly at all.

A few heavy steps took her to Madelyn's side. The first part of not scaring Madelyn would be not surprising her. The Coral Elf girl looked up and blinked her different colored eyes.

"Hello?" she whispered.

Raine smiled gently in response. "Hello, Madelyn. We've not really talked this semester. I think that's a shame."

The girl looked down. "I-I...sorry. I get that you're not a bully. It's just..." She sighed.

"It's okay. You're a freshman, and I'm a junior, and we're not in any of the same activities together. Now, I'm barely in any activities unless you count FBI training, and that's a special case, and there's no reason for you to even want to be involved in that." She managed to cut herself off in the middle of her inadvertent Christie impression.

"O-okay." Madelyn swallowed.

Raine kept a smile on her face, even though her heart sped up. Her panic grew. She was botching Operation Befriend Shy Coral Elf.

"Did you have a good break?" she asked to break the awkward silence. "Mine was okay, but most my hometown friends were gone, so it was a little boring."

"I don't...really have friends at home. Remember, it's a small place. You know, not a lot of people." Madelyn's gaze darted back and forth as if she didn't dare focus on Raine for more than a second. "I did things with Vianna. That's what I always do. And I slept a lot. It helps the time pass quicker."

Concern for the other girl eroded Raine's panic and worry. Vianna might be brusque, but she did her part to at least protect her sister. What were her parents doing? Their little girl was suffering, and both daughters had been so desperate that they had tried to contact sketchy wizards in the kemana.

"What about your parents?" she asked. She couldn't resist. Maybe she was butting her nose into someone else's business, but she'd done that from the minute she arrived at school. If she could help Madelyn by being Campbell the Busybody, so be it. At least helping her wouldn't involve taking on some dangerous magical enemy.

"My parents?" Madelyn sighed. "Um, they're...not there...a lot."

"They're not thinking of pulling you out of the school, are they?"

She shook her head. "No, no. It's not like that. It's... I don't know how to explain it." She swallowed, the entire motion obvious in her pale, delicate throat. "It's really only Vianna and me. As long as she looks out for me, I know I'll be okay."

Raine considered that, impressed by the length of the conversation. She must have made more of a positive impression on Madelyn last semester than she realized.

"It doesn't have to be only Vianna, you know." She smiled. "When I first came to this school, it was complicated. I'm an orphan. I have Uncle Jerry, but I didn't even know about my magical potential. It...well, it came out by accident, and I was scared. Then, I came here, and… I met good people and a few…less good people, but mostly good people."

"Less good people?"

"A few bullies."

Madelyn shivered, her eyes still downcast. "And how did you handle them?"

"I stood up to them." She shrugged. "I dealt with bullies back home, too. Just because the new bullies were magicals didn't make them any different."

"I wish I could be that confident." The elf looked up for a moment, her red eye and green eye filled with sorrow. She lowered her head. "But…I can't be."

"Not overnight, no, but you could learn to be."

Madelyn raised her palms and stared at them. "It's like magic on Earth, Raine. Some people are born with it. Some people aren't. I was born a miserable, scared coward. If it wasn't for Vianna, I don't know what I would do. I'd probably shrivel up and die."

"Don't talk like that. We all have our weaknesses." Raine shook her head firmly. "Friends can help with that. When I first came here, my boyfriend, Cameron, was different. He didn't trust people because of how shifters have been treated in the past, including him. My friend William—like you, he has a complicated relationship with his relatives, except they're Ifrit. My friend Philip was more obsessed with the next big thing than his friends and made some mistakes. Sara had a lot of trouble because her magic hadn't fully come in, and I was still learning to understand the world of magic when I first came here. Adrien has some crazy stuff in his past that weighed him down. It still does. And all my other friends have their own challenges. Everyone does, and the way they get through them is by relying on others."

"You don't understand," Madelyn whispered. "I can never be like you. I was born differently. My soul is different." She gasped, and her eyes widened as if she had imparted some great secret.

"Because you're a Coral Elf?" She sighed. "I'll admit I don't know much more about your people than what I've read. But I just told you, I'm friends with everyone from shifters to Ifrit. I refuse to believe that different races can't help each other in difficult times. That's all I'm offering, Madelyn."

"To join the FBI Trouble Squad?"

She chuckled. "I'll admit, a lot of that trouble is my fault. I simply don't know when to leave well enough alone."

"Like now?" the girl asked.

"I think being your friend is far less dangerous than taking on a dark druid or a strange magical VR game entity that's come alive."

Madelyn's breath caught. "Maeve." Her breathing grew shallow, and she grew so pale she would have had perfect arctic camouflage.

"Yes, Maeve." Raine frowned, puzzled by the reaction. "I didn't think you knew much about Arc Eighty-Eight."

"I...read about it on break."

"Well, I think about her from time to time. Maeve."

Madelyn jerked her head up, her eyes wide. "You do?"

She was surprised by the girl's reaction but kept her own expression calm. "Yes. I feel bad for her. I mean, what she did was wrong, but I understand now why she did it. In the end, she was lonely."

"Can you imagine what it was like?" Madelyn replied, her voice barely above a whisper. "To fear being trapped in a world where there's nothing real around you?"

Raine nodded. "Yes. That almost happened. We could have easily been trapped in Maeve's world if it weren't for the professors."

"I didn't mean it that way." The Coral Elf looked away. She trembled and wrapped her hands around her shoulders. "I meant for her. Maeve was...alive. She could think and feel, and she only wanted friends, but everything closed on her. Everyone left. So alone. So dark. So empty. Nothing left but her thoughts. Can you imagine what it'd be like?" She stared at nothing as if she could see the darkness closing in around her. "She had to contemplate what it would be like to be alone for eternity in nothingness with no one else there."

Raine stared at Madelyn and a chill ran through her. "No. It's not like that. She's gone. The professors checked. The government looked into it. Whatever Maeve was— whatever she created—collapsed. I feel sorry for her, but at least she didn't have to suffer."

The girl blinked several times. She squeezed her eyes closed. "I'm...sorry. I let my imagination get the better of me." She grabbed her book and shoved it into her flower backpack. Tears leaked from the corner of her eyes.

"Madelyn, I'm sorry. I didn't mean to upset you. I only wanted you to know I'm here if you ever need someone to talk to."

"It's not your fault." She grabbed her backpack and

stood. "It's not anyone's fault. It's simply the way the things are." She ran off, her backpack clutched in her hands, and tears streamed down her cheeks,

Raine stared after the girl, flabbergasted. Madelyn fleeing in tears wasn't new, but this time, it didn't seem like she was afraid of her. It was more like she felt excessive empathy for Maeve.

She felt bad for the girl, but excessive empathy at least meant she cared about others.

"I've reached out," she whispered quietly. "She knows that I'm willing to listen. Hopefully, she'll come and talk when she feels ready."

CHAPTER SIXTEEN

Thoughts of Madelyn's strange reaction lingered in Raine's mind as most of the FBI Trouble Squad headed toward a small room at 13 West Range in Charlottesville, Virginia. They were only missing Adrien because he was leading the Louper team in some extra practice. With the season going so well, he didn't want to miss out on the championship because they were lazy and too cocky toward the end.

The teens' trip up the street brought them to a black-and-white historical sign that explained the significance of the Raven Room. Poe's dorm nestled among others still in use. A red-brick, arched breezeway ran in front of the rooms, not all that far from the road and beyond the well-kept lawn.

Edgar Allan Poe (1809-1849)-writer, poet, and critic--was born in Boston, Mass. Orphaned at a young age, Poe was raised by John and Frances Allan of Richmond. He attended schools in England and Richmond before enrolling at the University of

Virginia on 14 Feb. 1826 for one term, living in No.13 West Range. He took classes in Ancient and Modern Languages. While at the university, Poe accumulated debts that John Allan refused to pay. Poe left the university and returned briefly to Richmond before moving to Boston in Mar. 1827. Some of his best-known writing includes *The Raven*, *Annabel Lee*, and the *Tell-Tale Heart*. He also edited the *Southern Literary Messenger* in Richmond from 1835 to 1837. Poe died in Baltimore, Md.

Raine frowned and peered up the street in the general direction of the Raven Room. "Do you sense that?" She looked at her companions.

"Magic," Sara murmured. "I haven't heard anything about the Raven Society being magicals."

Cameron stepped instinctively in front of Raine. "It might not have anything to do with them. It might be someone else looking to cause trouble."

Philip shook his head. "You all need to calm down, dudes." He looked around to make sure no one else was close. "It's not like there are no other magicals in town. Maybe someone simply used a spell to take pictures or something."

Raine wasn't sure. Her wand lay hidden in a pocket of the long coat she wore to fight off the still cool early March weather, but she didn't want to have to explain to Headmistress Berens why she was involved in a magical fight outside a historical site on a major college campus.

Sara cracked her knuckles. "If there is someone waiting for us, I say we go greet them. No one can mess with the True Cardinals."

Evie and William looked less enthused with the idea of a confrontation.

Raine marched across the lawn and directly toward the Raven Room, more eager to solve the mystery than fight anyone. Cameron and Sara hurried after her, and soon, the others fell in behind. They passed through an archway and made their way down the breezeway toward the room.

Wooden rocking chairs lined the area, one each in front of the dorm rooms. A college student with a backpack over her shoulder emerged from a room farther down. She glanced at them with a hint of derision for a moment before she turned and wandered off across the lawn.

The teens continued until they found the Raven Room. It wasn't hard with a huge plaque beside the door on the brick wall. A thick plexiglass sheet allowed a view inside but denied them direct access.

The interior was modest as one would expect of a preserved nineteenth-century dorm room—a bed, a writing desk, and a chair. There were certain amenities more indicative of the time period, including a fireplace. A chest stood near the back window and a raven statue stood on a nightstand.

The magic had only strengthened since they walked closer.

"Maybe it's extra defenses to protect the room," Philip said with a shrug. "They're doing that more and more at many historical places."

Raine rubbed her cheek and her eyes narrowed as she scanned the room in search of some hidden clue. "It could be, but perhaps it's another mystery. We should try a revelation spell."

Cameron shook his head. "There are probably cameras around we can't see, and I doubt there's some hidden magical mystery at the dorm room of one of the most famous authors in American history. That Raven Society comes here and does stuff. Someone would have noticed already."

Adrien scoffed. "I don't trust any group that names themselves after ravens."

The shifter shrugged. "They're only a bunch of literary nerds."

"Perhaps."

"Perhaps what?" asked a deep voice behind them.

The teens turned, expecting another college student. Instead, a dark-haired gnome stood expectantly as if waiting for an answer. He wore a hat like most gnomes they had seen, but rather than something more fashionable and modern, his was a top hat. It did pair well with his unbuttoned black velvet suit, gray vest, and black cravat. He looked like he'd stepped out of a portal from the nineteenth century as he rested his hands atop an onyx-tipped cane.

Raine smiled and decided to dodge the gnome's question by engaging with his fashion choices. "I take it you're a fan of Poe, judging by that outfit?"

He gave her a thin smile and gestured to his clothes "What? Isn't this what all the kids wear these days?" He pointed his cane up. Magic radiated off both the cane and the gnome.

She tensed.

"Don't worry," he said and lowered his cane. "I simply made it so no one can hear our conversation. I know you're from that magic school. You have that look. There's always a few of you who come each semester and poke around. Let me guess—you sensed magic from the room and wondered if a Tell-Tale Heart beats underneath? Perhaps a man bricked in a hidden compartment?"

Raine gave him a sheepish smile. "Well, not that."

Evie shuddered. "Gross."

Philip stared at the room. "Uh, is there? Or some raven with an attitude problem?"

The gnome laughed. "Of course not. Poe had a wonderful imagination, but those were only stories."

Cameron narrowed his eyes. "Magic used to be merely a story, too."

"That's true, my boy." He frowned. "My manners are atrocious. I should introduce myself. I'm Ted."

Philip laughed. "Ted? Seriously?"

Sara elbowed him.

The wizard gestured at the gnome. "I'm just saying, he's a gnome named Ted."

The gnome shrugged. "What's wrong with the name? It's short and easy to remember for most people."

William looked from the room to the gnome. "Are you a member of the Raven Society?"

Ted shook his head. "No, not as such. I'm nothing more than…you could say, a big fan of Edgar Allen Poe." He wandered to the plexiglass barrier. "Speaking of stories, do you know that some people claim Poe was an Oriceran?"

Raine shook her head. "I hadn't heard that. It's not mentioned on any of the promotional materials for this place."

"Was he?" Philip asked.

Ted shrugged. "Who can say? They claim he used magic to disguise himself as a non-magical human, and that some of his stories were inspired by unfortunate experiences with dark magic that he later came to regret. But not all. Let's not doubt the man's creativity, and obviously, some of his works don't lend themselves to arcane explanation. Some were simply products of a fertile mind exploring the world around him in a macabre and gothic fashion."

Raine wondered about *The Murders in the Rue Morgue.* Many critics disliked the end of the story because of the bizarre revelations concerning the identity of the killer. If the story was inspired by a magical incident, it might make more sense. Other Poe stories also lent themselves to suggestions of magical inspiration, such as *The Masque of the Red Death.*

The strange being in the story and the named disease were often dismissed as metaphors about the inevitability of death. But, based on what Raine had learned in her magical history class, stranger things had happened on Oriceran.

"Wait a minute." Sara marched forward and suspicion clouded her features. "If Poe was an Oriceran with magic, why would he die in Baltimore like some normal human?"

"Why indeed?" Ted replied with a thin smile. "But isn't his death considered rather mysterious? To this day, no one fully knows what happened." He shrugged. "Maybe it was like the end of 'Infinite Lighthouse.' Wouldn't that be a twist?" He reached into one of his pockets and fished out a small wooden raven. He held it out to Raine. "It always warms my heart when people appreciate Poe. Modern

Earth types, magical or not, have no appreciation for their past, even one as recent as a century or two."

Raine took the raven. She could sense minor magic from it. "What does it do?"

"Nothing, young lady. Nothing at all." Ted tipped his head and walked away. "Think of it as nothing more than a good luck charm."

William moved in front of Evie and his eyes blazed for a moment.

Raine looked sharply at him. "What's wrong?"

"Just give me a minute," he responded, his gaze locked on the retreating gnome. Once Ted had made it some distance away, William exhaled a sigh of relief. "That story he talked about—the lighthouse thing. Have you heard of it, Raine?"

She shook her head. "No, but it's not like I've read everything Poe has ever written. What about it?"

"I read about it when we decided to come here. Poe never finished the lighthouse story. Other authors have offered their versions, but there is no 'Infinite Lighthouse' out there by Edgar Allen Poe."

Raine gasped and looked for Ted, but he'd vanished. "Wait. You don't think that could have been *him*, do you?"

Cameron surveyed the area but found no trace of him. "I think he was only a weird gnome."

"You think, or you know?"

"I think we'll never know for sure."

CHAPTER SEVENTEEN

Adrien narrowed his eyes as his team wandered the narrow, circular cobblestone streets. Row after row of identical blue townhouses taunted the Louper team. They formed a maze of homes and also provided a continual source of surprise attacks by the angry human-sized and surprisingly fast multi-tentacled Venus Fly Trap monsters that constantly appeared.

It didn't help that the movie club had watched the 2024 remake of *Little Shop of Horrors* not all that long before. The elf was half-convinced the Louper officials had reached into his brain with magic to design the threats for the match, but he wouldn't let reminders about a silly musical sabotage them.

This was the quarter-finals match, and the Dallas Fire-flies were strong opponents. Any loss of concentration, however small, might lead to a loss. The Cardinals had worked too hard and come too far for that now.

The team moved in a loose diamond formation. Adrien was in the front, a sword in hand. Cody and Daniel manned the left and right sides, while Carlos and Jackson brought up the rear. They were still running their starting lineup for the match.

Something crashed through a window a little farther ahead. The team pivoted as a unit. Two Audrey IIs—as Adrien had taken to thinking of the monsters—slithered out of the living room on their twitching roots.

Cody and Daniel summoned fireballs with their wands. The harsh magic battered the monsters to good effect and set them ablaze. The captain tightened his grip on his sword as the burning plants continued their charge, but their flames soon overwhelmed them, and they collapsed.

More windows shattered nearby, and another wave of Audrey IIs emerged.

"Let's move," Adrien ordered. "The more time we waste fighting these plants, the more time the Fireflies have to close on the token. We also risk revealing our position at the same time."

The Cardinals jogged away from the house. From what they'd encountered in the first half of the match, the plant monsters tended to swarm areas where the team had killed one but would give up if a player was too far away.

A dozen houses later, the elf raised his hand to signal a halt. "We're far enough away. Now, we need a better plan before we continue."

Jackson frowned. "We have no clues and our tracking spells don't work. This isn't fair."

Adrien shook his head and gestured at the houses. "Do you notice anything?"

"No." Jackson pointed his wand at a house across the street. "They all look the same."

Carlson shook his head. "That's not true. The circle's getting smaller with each road. There used to be twenty houses per block but now, there are only seventeen. Somehow, though, we can't see the smaller number from a distance."

"Exactly." The captain looked back the way they had come.

The dark shapes of Audrey IIs lingered in the distance.

He pointed to the next street. "Sometimes, Louper's mostly a battle. Sometimes, it's mostly a puzzle, and at other times, Louper's mostly a race. We have to assume the Fireflies have realized the same thing—or are about to." He released the spell that supported his sword. "It's time to move. Don't burst. Let's save the magic for when we need it."

The Cardinals sprinted down the street with Adrien in the lead. He didn't try to cut through any narrow paths between the houses. It wasn't worth the risk of an ambush.

The air shimmered this time as they entered the next street, and the number of houses dropped by half. Oddly enough, the next street appeared to have the same number of houses as at the beginning of the match. Any effort to see through all the illusion spells was pointless. They merely needed to get to the center of the fake town.

His muscles and legs burned as he continued to pump his legs. There was no need to look back. He trusted that his team could keep up with him and knew they would. He had, after all, been the one to train them the entire season. Tactics, magic, and fitness were all key to a successful Louper team. Even Cody and Daniel had performed better than they had in previous seasons.

A bright flash in the distance was followed almost instantly by a peal of thunder. The Fireflies were near.

"Keep going!" Adrien shouted.

They were now down to six houses per block. Two shadows appeared from between some townhouses further down the street—Firefly players. They grinned and raised their wands but didn't point them at the Cardinals.

Small stones appeared in front of the opposing players' wands. A moment later, one of the rocks careened into a nearby window, crashed through, and left spider-webbed cracks across the glass. Another damaged a second window.

Cody and Daniel responded with a barrage of magic toward the Fireflies, but the opposing players ducked between the houses for cover. They darted out a moment later, only to shatter more windows.

The Audrey IIs took the bait to crash through the damaged panes or knock doors off their hinges as they emerged from the houses. Dozens flooded the street and surrounded the players.

"That was stupid," Jackson muttered. "They'll go down, too."

Adrien shook his head and summoned a new sword. "It was a sacrifice play."

"But Dallas hasn't tried one of those all season."

"Quarter-finals is as good a place as any for new strategies."

Cody, Daniel, and Carlos formed a triangle and began their fiery bombardment of the hungry mass of plant monsters that approached.

Jackson gritted his teeth. "We can't stay here. The other three Fireflies are probably on their way to the token."

"Burning them out is the best strategy." Cody launched another fireball.

"Jackon's right. We need to go." The captain pointed down the street and raised his sword. "We're carving our way through. Don't worry to finish them off, only to keep them off you. Ready?"

The team nodded, their game faces now solid steel.

The elf shouted a battle cry and hurtled forward. He summoned a second sword and used both with relentless precision. They made no attempt to hold their diamond formation this time but simply thrust ahead in a line of near-feral boys who raced headlong into a squirming mass of angry plant monsters.

Adrien met the front line of the Audrey IIs and slashed and swung his sword to separate tentacles from their attackers. Quick fireballs and bolts erupted all around, but Daniel switched tactics and summoned nets to quickly entangle the enemy. They wouldn't hold one of the tentacled monsters long, but they did a good job of slowing them.

The captain continued to cleave through the opposing ranks like the world's angriest gardener.

Carlos yelped as an Audrey II snatched his leg and yanked it out from under him. He lost his grip on his wand. "Sorry, Adrien. Keep going."

Adrien could only spare his teammate the briefest glance as his whirlwind assault continued. Cody adopted Daniel's strategy and they continued as more plants swarmed Jackson.

The Cardinals managed to push through the main horde. The three oldest players on the team switched from attacks to burst spells and launched themselves away from the monsters.

"The roofs," the elf ordered and dissipated his swords.

Rapid bursts raised them onto the roofs, and they continued to hop along the elevated route like the world's least-stealthy ninjas.

The end of the block forced them back onto the ground, but the air shimmered again and now, there was one house left. Unfortunately, three Louper players from the opposing team bolted toward it.

Cody and Daniel peeled away from Adrien and directed nets at the approaching Firefly players. The combatants immediately fried the nets with fire spells.

The elf released another burst, his jaw tight as the air rushed past his face. A few stray white bolts struck him and stung. He landed and rolled to his feet. Another burst spell hurled him through a second-floor window and glass erupted everywhere.

His shield protected him from injury, but the prize was nowhere in sight. He'd played in enough matches to know that if they didn't allow the players to track the token and didn't provide clues, it would be fairly obvious and out in the open. No one liked a Louper match that dissolved into slow-paced searching.

He had landed in a bedroom with a few bookcases, and a hasty examination of his surroundings confirmed that no gold was in sight. Frustrated, he flung the closet door open and tried to ignore the shouts and explosions outside. His search brought no results.

The elf rushed out of the room and into the hallway. A loud thump sounded from downstairs, but he once again blocked it out and flung himself into the next bedroom. It proved to be another futile exploration.

Adrien spared a quick glance over the second-floor banister as he hurried from the room. His breath hissed when he immediately saw the token on a coffee table in the living room, a Firefly player only yards away. An attack might not stop him in time given his defenses, especially since the match was about to end and restraint might not work. That left him with only one trick, and he could only hope it worked. He now regretted mocking the technique when he had compared notes with Raine about what had been taught in her section versus his earlier that semester.

"Not yet, Dallas," he shouted.

The Firefly player stumbled for a moment and gave the elf his opening. Adrien raised his hands and shouted an incantation for a spell he had honestly never taken seriously until that moment. Seconds later, slime coated his opponent from head-to-toe.

Blinded, the player stumbled forward and tripped to fall flat on his face.

The Cardinals caption vaulted over the banister and broke his fall with a quick air spell, but his knees still screamed at him in protest. He ignored the pain as his momentum hurled him toward the token.

His adversary raised his wand and cast an entangling spell. It took the form of thin nylon bolos, but the blinded wizard missed.

Adrien dropped to his knees on the hardwood floor and slid the last few feet toward the coffee table. He bumped into it and knocked the gold disc over the edge. It fell, and he caught it in midair.

As he stared at it, everything else seemed to recede in the distance. The token didn't only represent victory in the here and now. It represented victory in the quarter-finals and another win in an undefeated season.

It wasn't until the Louper environment vanished and the roar of the crowd in the stands sounded that the captain stood.

The Cardinals could do it. They could not only win the championship, but they could also have a perfect season.

CHAPTER EIGHTEEN

Evie, William, Raine, and Cameron smiled as they walked down a narrow street in Ruby Falls. The streets there always reminded Raine of a trip she once took to New Haven with Uncle Jerry. The lack of cars made for more irregular streets with more character.

The kemana was as busy as ever, filled with magicals of all types. Even if the population was much fewer than Charlottesville, the closeness of the buildings and the overall smaller area made it sometimes feel like the opposite. The overlapping chatter of different races, along with the sometimes extreme differences between them, only reinforced the feeling.

A cluster of pixies flew in tight formation over a lanky elf as they discussed the merits of a cleaning potion the elf had purchased from a local potions witch. A distressed Arpak woman stood on a corner and looked around, her wings folded tightly around her back.

Raine was about to go over and ask her what was

wrong when an Arpak man emerged from a nearby building, a lime-green paper bag in hand. The woman threw her arms around him and smiled.

"I guess she was only waiting for her boyfriend," Raine murmured.

"What was that? Cameron asked.

"Nothing. I only thought that not all boyfriends are as good as you."

He shrugged, a smug look of satisfaction on his face.

Three Light Elves speaking in their native tongue passed by the teens. To Raine's ears, their language sounded like complicated musical harmonies intertwined in a way that reminded her of intricate classical composition. She was so used to people speaking with translation spells that she often forgot all the wondrous diversity of Oriceran language.

"Too bad the others couldn't come," she said with a smile. "Although it's nice that Adrien is helping Christie out with some of her yearbook stuff. She's so busy this year, we barely get to see her."

"Sure, but Sara and Philip didn't need to make up that obvious excuse about studying together," Cameron said and rolled his eyes. "If they wanted some time alone, they could have simply asked for it."

Evie's warm smile had persisted since they had entered the kemana. "I think it's sweet. Everyone has someone now. Not that they necessarily needed someone, but all the relationships seem to make everyone happy."

William blushed and looked away.

The teens continued up the street. They didn't have a

particular location in mind, but they didn't want to visit any of their Charlottesville targets unless the whole crew was with them. Ruby Falls provided a pleasant alternative. Over the current school year, though, their affinity for Bubble and Fizz had lessened as they sought out slightly more sophisticated fare.

It made sense to Raine. The years had passed, and they were now close to their final year at the school. They weren't the same young, carefree teens who had started together and were almost adults. In some ways, they already were. Together, they had shared danger, true friendship, and love.

She exhaled a contented sigh.

Cameron flashed her a quick glance. "What's gotten into you? And should I be worried?"

"I'm thinking about everything that has happened these last couple of years."

"Thinking more about the past than the future?"

Raine nodded. "Something like that."

She stared at a cart selling Oriceran plants. Several of them twitched and moved and reminded her of the monsters the Cardinals had faced during their quarter-finals match. Some magicals liked to buy those types of plants as pets, but she couldn't help but find them creepy. Too much *Little Shop of Horrors.*

"Move. Step aside—get out of the way!" a voice shouted from a nearby narrow alley.

A familiar unusually large ferret in a red top hat and vest emerged—none other than Horatius A. Pierce. His satchel was slung over his shoulder. The ferret raced down the street, headed in the teens' general direction. They'd only been in the kemana a couple of times that semester, but they hadn't seen him. Raine had thought that he had possibly moved on after the disappointments in his short-lived entertainment management career.

She immediately drew her wand and expected angry Willen to emerge from the alley, but no one came out after the creature.

"Hap!" she called.

The ferret skidded to halt and blinked at her. He removed his top hat and bowed over it. "Greetings, salutations, and hello, young lady. It's been far too long."

Cameron glanced back and forth, suspicion and concern on his face. Fire flashed in William's eyes, and he also kept watch for enemies. Evie slid her hand into her pocket to finger a few of the potions she always carried with her. They weren't the FBI Trouble Squad because they were unprepared.

"Are you all right, Hap?" Raine asked.

He nodded and flipped his hat back on his head. "Yes, I've never been better."

"But you were running."

Hap patted the satchel strap. "Of course, because I'm now a delivery ferret. Fastest whiskers in Ruby Falls, I'll tell you that. Good, honest work. It doesn't involve the Red Coat Society or ungrateful Sirens." He gave her a little salute. "Unfortunately, as much as I am grateful, thankful, and appreciative of your previous help, I have a delivery to make. I'll see you kids around." The ferret scurried off and his tail twitched behind him.

Raine blinked. "That was…brief."

Evie laughed and withdrew her hand from her pocket.

Cameron grinned. "He finally has an honest job. Good for him."

"The job for the Siren was honest, even if she wasn't," William reminded them and shook his head.

Raine's stomach rumbled. "I'm a little hungry. Why don't we try that new seafood place we saw last time?"

"That sounds good," the shifter said.

They emerged from the restaurant, full and happy. The food was delicious and reasonably priced. Raine tried to remember if she had ever had a bad meal in Ruby Falls.

Two men and a woman in dark suits talked quietly with some of the local residents across the street. They wore sunglasses, which was unnecessary in the kemana. The glowing light of the roof always illuminated the area, but it wasn't the blinding light of the sun.

"Who are they?" she asked. "They look suspicious."

Cameron shook his head. "Raine, don't go looking for trouble. The police can handle it if there is trouble."

"Paranormal Defense Agency," replied a woman nearby and suspicion clouded her tone. "They showed up a couple of days ago. They've asked if anything strange has happened around here, but they won't tell anyone what it's about. Instead, they insist that it's a 'routine safety investigation.'" She snorted. "Government agents looking for magicals to harass, I bet."

"But they're wizards and witches," she replied. "They're magicals, too."

The woman shook her head. "Sometimes, I think I liked things better when magic wasn't out in the open and the government wasn't always breathing down our neck." She harrumphed and walked up the street.

Raine sighed and looked at her friends. "And sometimes, I forget that not everyone looks up to federal law enforcement like I do."

"Add it to your reasons for joining the FBI," Cameron said. "Catching bad guys and bridging the magical and non-magical gap are good enough reasons but helping resolve some of the suspicion magicals feel toward the government is another good one."

One of the PDA agents nodded to a man and handed him a card before moving inside an herbalist's shop.

William's eyes narrowed. "I've never heard of the PDA doing routine safety inspections. I think they're lying about why they're here."

Raine's heart sped up. "Do you think we should investigate, after all?"

Cameron frowned. "That's the PDA. If there is any trouble in the kemana, they'll be able to handle it better than a bunch of students. Let it go, Raine."

She hesitated for a moment. A part of her wanted to challenge her boyfriend, but he was right. She couldn't think of anything she could offer an investigation that federal law enforcement magicals couldn't also provide.

Raine sighed and shrugged agreement. "Should we head back?"

Evie nodded. "I need to talk to Tori about a few things anyway."

They turned away from the PDA agents and walked up

the street. Their route brought them to an intersection sandwiched between four distinct restaurants, all with dragon in their names. Raine remembered the places having different names and decor the last time she visited, but restaurants failed as often in the kemana as they did in the non-magical world. Turnover, in and of itself, wasn't unusual but it wasn't normally so quick and spectacular.

A tall senior from their school emerged from the closest restaurant, Dragon's Breath. Caleb, the current president of the Art Club, carried a small brown bag in hand and wore an easy smile.

Raine had talked to him a few times, but he was more Sara's friend than hers. She waved to be polite.

He approached the four friends. "It's rare to see you all out and about without the other three."

"They had things to take care of," she explained.

Caleb raised the bag. "If you see Sara before I do, let her know I found the art supplies we talked about." He beamed happily. "There's nothing like a good trip to the kemana to refresh my muse."

"We'll let her know." She glanced over her shoulder. "You wouldn't happen to know anything about why the PDA is here, would you?"

The smile faded from his face, replaced by confusion. "The PDA? No. I didn't even know they were here. Has something happened?"

"Not that I know of. I was curious, that's all."

Cameron sighed. "Let it go, Raine."

"It doesn't hurt to ask."

Caleb shrugged. "Sorry. I wish I could be more help."

"No, it's okay. It's only me being curious. Don't worry

about it. We're headed back to the school. Were you on your way?"

"Yes, I was."

She gestured with her arm. "Please, join us."

"I'd be happy to."

CHAPTER NINETEEN

Raine had numerous FBI training sessions with Agent Connor throughout the semester. She'd always been able to focus, but she couldn't that afternoon. While the FBI agent explained the intricacies of the grand jury process, Raine's thoughts returned constantly to the PDA agents in the kemana.

Her instructor frowned. "Raine?"

She blinked and refocused on him. "Yes?"

"Have you even been listening? I don't think you've heard a single thing I've said in the last few minutes."

Raine glanced at William, who gave her a sympathetic look.

"Sorry," she said and smiled sheepishly. "I'm distracted because I can't help but think about the PDA agents in the kemana."

Agent Connor's face tightened. "PDA agents?"

Her breath caught, and she leaned forward. All these FBI training sessions definitely had helped. He clearly knew something. His body language screamed it.

"What's going on?" she asked and kept her voice even and calm without a hint of accusation in it. "If there's a threat to the school, the students deserve to know. The history of this place shows that keeping us in the dark doesn't keep us safe."

William grimaced. "Raine!"

The agent raised a hand and shook his head to still the protest. "No, William. It's fine. It's important that you both trust me." He fixed his attention on Raine. "I'll tell you, but I don't want you to spread it around the school. The head-mistress doesn't want a panic over something that might not even happen."

"I think we've proven that we can keep a secret, Agent Connor."

He grinned. "Yes, you have," he agreed, but his grin morphed slowly into a frown. "The PDA is in Ruby Falls because they have reason to believe a dangerous magical fugitive may be coming there—someone who is near the top of the DHS Enhanced Threats list."

"Eris!" Raine shouted.

Agent Connor stared at her, surprise written on his face. "You know about her?"

"They might restrict my access to the outside world when I'm on school grounds, but I can still access the Internet during the breaks. I've used the public libraries in Charlottesville, too. The FBI Most-Wanted and the DHS Enhanced Threats lists are all matters of public record. I check them whenever I can."

William scrubbed a hand over his face. "Sometimes, I feel like a distant second when it comes to wanting to be an FBI agent. I don't even think to do that kind of thing during a break."

Their instructor chuckled. "It wasn't what I did when I was your age." He sobered and nodded. "Yes, Raine. The PDA has reason to believe Eris is coming to Ruby Falls, but they've tried to keep it somewhat low-key because they don't want to scare her off. If you've followed her career at all, you know how hard it is to predict her movements."

"Low-key?" Raine shook her head. "If random students from the school were able to see them questioning people on the street, I'm sure some fugitive witch would definitely hear about it long before they saw her."

"You're not wrong, but I personally like the idea. I don't want Eris anywhere near this school or the students, if possible."

"I don't get it." She frowned, a little perplexed. "Aren't the PDA tracking her directly? That's how they know she's coming, right?"

"No. This involves more old-fashioned law enforcement methods, including witnesses."

"Huh. I get that she's probably warded, but Hudson told us that, in a few weeks, we'll start a unit on advanced tracking. Apparently, with enough magicals helping out, you can get through anti-tracking wards."

Agent Connor shook his head. "I'm not a magical expert, but I do know that falls more under the category of generally true than absolutely true. Do you know about her background?"

"Only the stuff the FBI and PDA have mentioned."

"Then you know about the artifact?"

Raine nodded.

William sighed. "Should I write all this down?"

"No," the agent said. "This is a PDA case, and they handle things differently." He turned to Raine. "The same artifact that strengthened Eris' magic also, for whatever reason, made her immune to tracking magic. From what I've been told, she only uses wards to confuse government attempts to track her. There's no easy magical way to know where she's coming from or going to."

"Wow." Raine whistled appreciatively. "She really is the Witch Queen of Chaos."

The half-Ifrit frowned. "Then she might be coming. She might already be in the kemana, hiding out and waiting for her chance to do whatever her plan is."

"That's true, but that's also the PDA's responsibility." Agent Connor folded his arms over his chest. "And it doesn't matter. Eris might be powerful and effectively immune to tracking, but that's not the same thing as being immune to all magic. From everything the headmistress has told me about the wards, there's absolutely no way Eris could hope to get into this place without the staff knowing. That means the worst thing that might happen to you all is that you're restricted to school grounds for a few days."

Raine nodded and worked hard to keep the eagerness off her face. She couldn't help it. The opportunity to help apprehend the chaos witch was the ultimate temptation.

The trainer unfolded his arms and walked over to tap a grand jury flow chart. "But let's focus on the FBI, not the PDA. This information's important. Knowing how prosecutors utilize information in indictment proceedings will help you to better information collect and investigate crimes as a field agent. Of course, bureau procedures should guide everything, but understanding what under-pins those procedures will still help."

Both students nodded. For Raine, merely knowing Eris might be coming satisfied the curiosity that had eaten away at her. Now that she had her answers, it was simply a matter of waiting to see if the Witch Queen of Chaos showed up.

CHAPTER TWENTY

Adrien stood in front of the eight other members of the Louper team. They were gathered on the field and arrayed in a line, and their stern expressions matched his—almost more like soldiers than players.

"As I told you at last practice," he began, "just because we have some time before the semi-finals doesn't mean we can slack off. Louper might be a simulation, but it's a simulation that reflects our actual reality. The more we improve ourselves outside the game, the better we'll perform inside the game. That is why conditioning and practice are still necessary. Today, though, we'll focus on improving some of our entangling spells. The quarter-finals match revealed that we're a little too focused on mobility and damage as part of our offensive strategy. I don't want to lose our shot at the championship because we're not flexible enough."

The team members all nodded, and the serious looks remained. Everyone felt the pressure of their undefeated season. Their hard work had brought them this far, but in the weeks leading up to semi-finals, they would need to train even harder.

Most people talked about hunger and wanting it. Adrien didn't like that attitude. Success didn't go to people because they *wanted* it. Success came because people earned it through effort.

"Everyone, pair off," he ordered. "One partner will work on entanglement. The other partner will work on countering it. Then you'll switch. Vary it up. Remember that every technique you can think of can be countered. We need to train hard so we don't have to think in battle, and we need to train twice as hard after that so we can automatically change our tactics without even having to discuss it as a team." He pointed to Cody and Daniel. "Exactly like they did in the quarter-finals. That's what comes from experience, and it's what let us win our match."

The two wizards jumped into the air for a chest bump. Apparently, a high-five wouldn't do.

The captain's drill sergeant persona faded for a second as he smiled at their enthusiasm. Losing them at the end of the year would hurt the team, but there was a lot of up-and-coming talent. Even if they lost the championship match this year, he hoped he had done a good job as captain and hadn't let down either his brother or the old captain, Matt.

"Let's get going." Adrien clapped his hands together.

Cody and Daniel paired off. Carlos and Jackson partnered while Hilda joined Dennis, and the remaining two freshmen formed the final pair.

"We'll start at twenty yards," the elf explained. "Then,

we'll move closer with each round. Alternate between the two of you."

Daniel started with a conjured chain. As a senior, his magic was more controlled and refined than most of the other players, and Adrien doubted the underclassman could achieve that type of entanglement with such ease.

Cody didn't even blink as he shouted his incantation, his wand already pointed at his partner. A blinding white orb struck the chain and severed it into two pieces. The heavy metal links missed him narrowly on either side before they vanished.

The elf frowned. "Everyone, put a shield up just in case. Remember, this is Louper training, but we're still in the real world."

He strolled up and down the field and watched his team members exchange and parry enchantments. Carlos fell to vines. Dennis narrowly avoided Hilda's rope only to get stuck when she turned the ground into mud beneath him and hardened it. Everyone breathed hard now, and sweat sheened their faces.

"You're doing good," Adrien shouted. "Keep it up. But remember, there are different ways to defend yourself. It's one thing to stop the attack, but you can also simply get out of the way. Cody and Daniel are the only ones who've done much bursting. I know a lot of you don't have as much experience with it, but the only way you'll get better is if you use it."

With other regional quarter-finals still to be played, the

Cardinals didn't yet know who they would face in the semi-finals, so it was critical that they maintain flexibility. Every team had their strengths and weaknesses, and being able to exploit them, even in a magical VR environment, meant understanding them in the real world.

The captain approached the two wizards. "Cody, why don't you take a break so I can get some practice in?"

Cody wiped the sweat off his forehead and nodded. He stepped away from Daniel as Adrien jogged about fifteen yards away from him.

The elf summoned a sword and gestured for the wizard to make his move.

Daniel turned away, whipped back toward his opponent, and rattled off a quick spell. His eyes widened in surprise and he grunted as he burst backward. He collided with Hilda, and she yelped in alarm. They tumbled and rolled in a tangle of limbs.

Adrien blinked and released his sword, confused. Everyone else stopped their exercises and headed over toward their downed teammates.

The two players extricated themselves from one another. Their shields, fortunately, had saved them from serious injury.

"What happened?" the captain asked. "I didn't pay close attention, but it sounded more like an entanglement incantation and nothing like a burst at all."

The spells weren't even that similar. Someone would have to deliberately try to cast the other spell.

Daniel frowned and shook his head. "That's what I thought I did. I don't know. The plan was to immobilize you with a net, but for some reason, it came out as an air burst instead." He reclaimed his wand from where it had fallen, his brow furrowed in confusion and irritation.

Adrien glanced at Cody. "What did you hear?"

"It sounded like an entanglement spell to me." The wizard shrugged.

"I honestly don't know what happened." Daniel frowned belligerently at his wand.

The elf hissed. "I know."

"You do?"

"I've run you all ragged." He frowned. "Mistakes are bound to happen. Practice is important, but so is rest. We won't win if we're exhausted and don't execute our spells correctly."

"Maybe." Daniel sighed and shook his head. "Sorry, Adrien."

"It's not your fault. I'm the captain. It's my fault." He nodded toward the main mansion. "That's enough practice for today. We'll take a few days off. Relax. We have time before the next match."

Everyone nodded but still regarded Daniel and Hilda with concern. The players filed off the field, including Daniel who still scowled at his wand.

"I'll catch up with you," Cody called to him. "I have to talk to Adrien for a second."

"Okay." He continued to study his wand will real bewilderment

The wizard approached Adrien when the others were out of earshot. "I'm telling you, Adrien, that wasn't a burst spell. It wasn't even close. We didn't even use the Louper gear, so it's not like it's some sort of glitch."

"You don't have to defend him, Cody. It's like I said. I don't blame him for the failure of my leadership."

"I'm only saying it's weird, is all."

"It's magic." The elf chuckled. "Sara once brought cupcakes to life by accident. No matter how well we drill and train, magic is still magic. It can have a mind of its own when we're not focused. I don't think Daniel said the wrong thing. I think he's tired, like we are all are, and didn't have the right focus." He pointed at himself. "We're so close to the championship. I've put almost everything aside and even spent less time with my girlfriend. I think I've developed a little tunnel vision. A few days off won't hurt us. Matt always knew when to push and when to let us relax."

The wizard didn't look convinced, but he nodded. "If you say so, and I want to be clear, Adrien." He stuck his hand out. "Whether we take the championship or not, you've been an awesome captain. You've done Matt proud. We all feel that way."

"Thanks, Cody." Adrien reached over and shook the boy's hand.

Cody turned and jogged after the now distant Daniel.

It had to be fatigue. There was no way the wizard would have screwed up a spell he had cast hundreds, if not thousands of times.

The captain looked over the practice field. Maybe he was wrong about Louper. Maybe it did come down to who wanted it more.

CHAPTER TWENTY-ONE

Sara smiled as she dabbed her brush against her palette. Her latest painting, a somewhat abstract representation of the Raven Room, had come along nicely. She'd infused a little magic into the canvas that would help some of the shadows adjust themselves at random.

It was a subtle manipulation, but it did add to the atmosphere. She normally didn't try for anything creepy or unsettling, but a Poe-themed painting didn't seem to call for her normal beauty focus.

Jillian stepped into the art room and her gray eyes scanned back and forth. The Gray Elf nodded to herself as if satisfied that they were alone before she headed toward the other girl.

Sara set her brush and palette on a nearby table. She doubted that Jillian had come to ask about a painting. The Gray Elf junior was a member of the Live Unnecessary Tricksters, and she'd never expressed much interest in art.

"Can I help you?" she asked.

Jillian raised her hands and whispered a spell.

The kitsune frowned. "What did you do?"

"Privacy barrier. This is Trickster business. No one else needs to know."

Sara almost rolled her eyes. As fun as last year's prank war had been, she still found the Tricksters' obsession with pretending they were a secret society silly. Even most of the freshmen knew all their members.

"What's up?" she asked and kept a pleasant smile on her face.

"April 1st is coming soon," Jillian intoned, utter solemnity on her face. "It's time for the Second Annual Trickster Prank War. We need to prepare." She withdrew a small clay figurine from her pocket. "I even got this out of storage."

"What is that, exactly?"

The elf blinked. "I suppose I never did tell you. It's an artifact that suppresses my precognitive powers. A proper prank war should involve magic but not precognition." She slipped the figurine back into her pocket. "There's no challenge if there's no surprise."

"Oh." Sara nodded. She'd thought about the coming prank war on and off, but for some reason, the dates hadn't registered in her mind.

It had also honestly never occurred to her that Jillian shouldn't have been surprised by as many pranks as she had been last year given her Gray Elf precognition. Every different race had their quirks, and sometimes, it was hard to remember that while many races looked mostly humanoid, they weren't necessarily all the same.

"You will participate, right?" The girl raised her chin, a strange mix of desperation and aloof pride still in her eyes. "We know that you're more comfortable as an honorary member of the Tricksters, but your utter defeat of us last year calls for revenge. We wouldn't be satisfied if we didn't have a chance to pay you back."

Sara sighed. "I'm not saying I don't want to do it, but I also think a straightforward prank war might be a little too…boring."

Jillian jerked back as if struck, her mouth agape. "Boring?"

"Yes." She shrugged. "I know we'll try to be creative with the pranks, but if it's the same basic thing, don't you think it won't be as much fun?"

Panic spread across her companion's face. "The Second Annual Trickster Prank War is first and foremost a challenge of skill, but what's the point of a Trickster activity that would be…" She gritted her teeth. "Uh…boring?"

"Just saying." The kitsune folded her arms over her chest. "We need to mix it up a little."

"Pranks in town?"

"No to that one. Headmistress Berens would probably shove us into the World in Between if we perform magical pranks in town."

"The kemana, maybe?"

"So the kemana police can arrest us? I'm sure the headmistress would love that as well," Sara snapped. "But that does give me an idea."

Hope returned to Jillian's eyes. "You're the winner of the last prank war. Any ideas you have on how to improve the next one would be welcome. I'll take them to Kenneth, and I'm sure he'll agree."

"The problem with pranksters going after pranksters is that they think too much alike." Sara lowered her arms and laughed. "Even me, and I wasn't much of a prankster before. I suppose you guys were right about my kitsune blood."

The elf nodded. "That all makes sense, but I don't understand how it helps us."

"We need non-pranksters as opponents. People who are smart and like to investigate things, but who won't see through the pranks as easily. Of course, they also have to be good enough sports that they won't be angry if they are pranked."

Jillian frowned. "But you'd need the spirit of a Trickster to properly compete. We can't find anyone like you describe."

Sara wagged a finger. "I actually know two people whom I think might be interested."

"Two? Who?"

"Raine and William."

Her companion's frown deepened. "They don't have the spirits of Tricksters."

The kitsune shook her head. "No, but they're both training to be FBI agents. Think about it. This is the ultimate showdown of order versus chaos. Isn't that half the point of being a Trickster? Raine even briefly mentioned to me last year that she liked the idea of a 'cops versus robbers' prank war. I didn't think much of it at the time, but now, I really like the idea."

"Go on." Jillian's expression softened as she warmed to the idea.

"The way I see it, we have a three-way prank war. Basically, because I'm the reigning champion, I'll take all of you on. Then, we have our two trainee agents trying to stop everyone. Maybe they'll involve the rest of the FBI Trouble Squad, too." Sara grinned. "If we're as good at pulling pranks as we're supposed to be, having a few non-Trickster opponents should only increase the challenge."

The Gray Elf's breath caught at the word challenge. She obviously liked the idea. "We'll need to iron the details out."

"That's fine. I've simply thrown the general idea out there. I want the prank war to be fresh."

Jillian nodded and headed toward the door. "I'll find Kenneth right away and talk to him. This will be a truly epic battle. We'll earn our revenge against you and we'll show that the Tricksters can beat even the FBI."

Sara laughed. She didn't know if beating Raine and the rest of her friends counted as beating the FBI, but if that was what got the girl fired up, there was no reason to question it.

CHAPTER TWENTY-TWO

Everyone sat around two tables situated close together in the dining hall for their dinner. Sara used her fork to pull a piece of halibut off.

Tonight's ceiling was rather unexotic by kitchen pixie standards—a cloud-filled sky with patches of blue sneaking through on occasion.

"So when Jillian came back," Sara continued, "she explained the basic idea—that they want to make it fun for them and fun for Team FBI. They came up with a few ideas for that."

William and Raine both nodded

Philip looked a little uncomfortable as he slurped spoonfuls of his soup. Maybe the pixies had messed their spicing up.

Adrien watched the conversation in complete silence. Every once in a while, he glanced around in search of Christie. She had said she might not be able to come to dinner with him because of some last-minute interviews. Her efforts on the yearbook, as far as Raine could tell, individually dwarfed all the effort put in by last year's Year-book Club members combined.

"What are the rules?" Raine asked.

Sara nodded. "I'm glad you asked. The rules would be that everyone doing pranks, including me, would give Team FBI clues so they—that is, you—can investigate and have a chance to stop them." She took a bite of her fish.

Raine took a deep breath and her heart rate kicked up. The whole idea sounded fun, and it would give her something to do before Eris showed up and she tracked the witch down in the kemana.

The more she thought about it, the more convinced she felt that she could do exactly that. She didn't intend to confront the witch by herself, but if she could find her, she could at least point the PDA at her. After that, she could emphasize how her *FBI* training had helped her locate the witch. The prank war would be a nice warm-up.

"And how do we determine who wins?" she asked.

The kitsune swallowed. "Everyone who pulls a prank off successfully will get a point, and Team FBI will get points for preventing them. Whoever has the most points by the end of the war on April 1st wins."

William frowned. "We can't spend all day trying to stop that many people, though. Even if it's the weekend, it could still be dozens."

Sara shook her head. "The idea is that we start a week or so before the 1st. It won't be this massive wave, then. We'll spread them out, but April 1st will still be special."

"How?"

"The pranks will all count for double points on that day, but each Trickster, including me, will only be allowed one.

If scores are close, that should give both teams a chance to pull ahead."

Raine considered the explanation before she nodded quickly. "Which means there are seven possible pranks on the 1st. That's still a lot for two people to stop."

"You can get the rest of them to help, too." Sara gestured around the table. "The Tricksters don't care. I think they like the idea of a challenge. They want this is to be a fair fight, and so do I. If you don't feel comfortable with anything, we can adjust the rules."

"I guess if we split up and focus on different clues, it won't be so bad. Even if William and I do the main problem solving, having more people to send out gives us more of a chance to stop them. I think we can do this. It's not like a normal crime. We'll have clues before anything even happens, which means we'll have a good chance to prevent them."

Evie sighed and looked down. She didn't look all that happy about the idea of participating.

Adrien paid more attention to his steak than he did to the conversation.

Philip looked on the verge of panic, which confused Raine, but she didn't want to embarrass him by pointing it out.

"What do you think?" Sara asked.

William frowned, still a little thoughtful. "I don't understand something. Are you your own team? You made it sound like it was a three-way battle before."

"I am, but I also am not. Some of the pranks the Tricksters plan will target me, but my own pranks count as part of Team Trickster. Plus, each individual accumulates points. Otherwise, I'd be at a big disadvantage if I tried to battle both the Tricksters and Team FBI." The kitsune smirked. "I might be able to pull it off, but I'll take the handicap for this year's prank war."

Raine rubbed her hands together. "I like it. I think it's fair, and I think Team FBI has a good chance at winning." She eyed Sara. "You're our main competition. The Tricksters are a little too cocky, so I bet William and I will see right through them. They have experience with pranks, but they've never faced us before. They'll see what we've learned from Agent Connor."

Cameron grinned. "You've been dying to investigate something all semester, so you'll take a prank war if you can't get a real criminal?"

"I think of it like sparring. I need something to keep my skills fresh. The PDA might be in the kemana, but everything's still quiet down there. Even Hap's staying out of trouble."

The only other real lead Raine had was Madelyn and Vianna's trouble, but that wasn't a crime. That was merely parents who didn't care enough, and that wasn't anything she could help with. She'd run into Madelyn a few times and they had chatted briefly, but the girl was obviously uncomfortable, so Raine kept the conversations short for her sake.

"I'm not complaining, Raine," Cameron replied. "I'm glad something will keep you busy before you go looking for something more dangerous to investigate. I'll help out. Maybe a shifter nose will be useful. Who knows?"

Philip eyed him. "Did you do that on purpose, dude?"

"Do what?"

"Shifter nose. Who knows?"

Cameron snort-laughed. "Nope. That wasn't on purpose, but it doesn't change anything."

"Great, so we have a good starter Team FBI with you, William, and me." Raine almost bounced in her seat.

The half-Ifrit cleared his throat. "Shouldn't I have a say in whether I'll participate? There are a lot of assumptions here about these teams."

Everyone looked at him.

Raine had assumed he would be as eager as she was, but as he had pointed out during their discussion of Eris with Agent Connor, he didn't spend as much time obsessing over the FBI as she did. He obviously wanted to join the agency, so she didn't hold it against him. After all, it was an honorable job to him, but it represented a family legacy to her.

She didn't want to push him, but she wasn't certain she could win without him either—not against the entire Live Unnecessary Tricksters and Sara.

"You don't want to? I really do think it's a good way to practice investigation skills, but you don't have to if you don't think you'll enjoy it. I think everybody involved wants it to be fun." She sighed but tried to smile through her disappointment.

William shrugged and grinned. "All I said is that I wanted a say in whether I participate. I agree with you, and I do want to join Team FBI. We'll leave the Tricksters crying."

Sara laughed. "Dramatic much? We have William, Cameron, and Raine, so we have the beginning of a Team FBI."

Relief flooded Raine. As much as she loved Cameron and valued his assistance, he hadn't received the kind of investigation training that William had. Despite the arrogance displayed by the Tricksters in the past, the final scores might end up close.

"Oh, I forgot," the kitsune said. "The official end of the war will be 5:00 PM on April 1st. The way I see it, this will a be a fun distraction before we have to start worrying about the Spring Formal. Who else is in?"

Adrien shook his head. "I still need to focus on Louper practice."

Evie sighed. "Sorry, William. The more I think about it, the more I don't think I'd like it."

He smiled. "It's fine."

Sara turned to Philip, an expectant smile on her face.

The wizard threw his hands up. "Don't hate me, Sara, but I can't participate. I promised a couple of different organizations I would do more volunteer work at the end of March and beginning of April. I meant to tell you, but I kept forgetting."

She smiled at him. "I won't be mad that you're doing volunteer work, Philip."

The boy sighed with relief.

"Okay, then." Raine licked her lips. "Team FBI is me, William, and Cameron. It's a smaller team than I had hoped for, but I still think we can do it." She offered a hungry grin to Sara. "You tell Kenneth it's on."

CHAPTER TWENTY-THREE

The first day of the great and glorious team-based Second Annual Trickster Prank War wouldn't start for several days, so it didn't occupy Raine's thoughts as she settled in for the beginning of a new spell unit with Professor Hudson.

The professor's class was one of the few in which almost the entire FBI Trouble Squad was present in the same section that semester. Cameron, of course, didn't take the class, but everyone else was there.

Professor Hudson cleared her throat. She held her wand in front of her with both hands. "Today, we begin our new advanced tracking class. Previously, you've been taught tracking, and most of you have gained an acceptable level of proficiency. In common scenarios, this is sufficient. A lost item, pet, or person generally wants to be found, so your basic tracking spell will be enough." She smiled. "It's one of the reasons unsolved missing person cases have plummeted in recent years. Although most police departments only have limited access to magic, they generally at least have some sort of contract with magicals to help with search and rescue."

Adrien frowned in the second row.

She gestured to him. "Is there a problem?"

"How do non-magicals criminals ever escape, then? If they always have a witch, wizard, or Oriceran to help, criminals should never get away."

"An astute observation." The professor sighed. "There are multiple issues at play. Police departments also have limited resources and some legal restrictions in terms of recovering criminals using magic. I'm not a lawyer, so I don't understand all the fine details, but it can make it difficult for them in certain cases if they've tracked a criminal down directly using magic. In addition, the expense isn't always worth it. Many departments want to make sure they save such resources for true missing persons cases and the like. But the third reason is related to the advanced tracking technique unit we'll begin studying."

The elf frowned. "Criminals have money and magic, too. If they ward themselves or hire someone to ward them, they can block tracking."

"Exactly. As this is not a dark magic defense issue, I'll teach this, rather than Professor Powell, but some of the underlying educational logic is the same." Professor Hudson raised her wand and made a few intricate movements. An image of a young witch pinned beneath a huge flooring stone appeared. "There's also the non-criminal possibility of a magical getting trapped in an already warded location."

"Like the School of Necessary Magic," William said.

"Again, exactly. Although most of the wards only block

people tracking from outside the school grounds, rather than internally." Professor Hudson waved her wand again. A globe replaced the trapped witch. "Very powerful magicals outside the grounds could attempt to trace any of you, and they would be unable to find you, even with the advanced techniques we'll learn." She cut through the air with her wand, and the image disappeared. "Note that it's also not simply a matter of the wards. It's also a question of the level of background magic."

Raine raised her hand.

"Yes, Raine?"

"I don't understand what the level of background magic has to do with it."

"You have to understand that part of tracking is homing in on the essence of what you're tracking." She pointed her wand at the girl. "When you're a magical, that inherent magic is the easiest aspect of a person to track. Remember, back when the gates were still closed, it was entirely possible to easily track a person using magic all the way across the world, simply because they used magic. Now, though, even if the gates will take thousands of years to open fully, there's enough background magic that such easy tracking is no longer possible. There is too much noise. That same background magic also makes it slightly harder to track any magical accordingly."

The students all nodded and a few took notes. Most had heard these concepts before, but it was good to hear a refresher.

Professor Hudson's smile faltered for a moment. "It is the official position of this school that you need to know how to do magic to the utmost level of your ability, regardless of the spell. There are various possible reasons why you might want to use this, but now that we've gone over some background, we will focus strictly on the spell itself." She looked around the room. "This is where things can get difficult. For one thing, beating wards or other types of anti-tracking requires some sort of physical focus. The strongest focus is a physical part of the person—hair is a common choice—but possessions with great emotional connection to the target can also be helpful. I trust you can sacrifice a few hairs for your education."

The class laughed.

"Note also that this advanced tracking spell is difficult to cast in many ways. The most common way is to use a container filled with water and a needle. The spell causes the needle to float, and it works as a sort of tracking compass, but it doesn't provide much in the way of distance information. It is also very distance sensitive, so if you attempt to track someone in a heavily warded area, you would need to be close to even begin."

Juniper raised her hand. "How close?"

"It's not as if there's a specific recorded distance. Let's say, in general, if you attempt to track someone in a warded area, you would probably want to be in the same city to have a chance of finding them."

A murmur swept through the class. Raine wasn't surprised as she had already read about some of these limitations, but many students at the school reacted poorly whenever they ran into a limit of magic. Perhaps being raised thinking she didn't have magic predisposed her to accept such limits.

Professor Hudson pointed to a water-filled glass with a

needle at the bottom on the nearest table. "You've all been provided the necessary implements. We'll make this easy. Today, you won't be able to complete the spell successfully, but we'll practice. In a few days, we'll play a little game of hide and seek."

Raine gripped her glass in one hand and her wand in the other as she crept down the hallway. Every few steps required her to wait a few seconds for the water to settle. She frowned as the needle spun abruptly in the opposite direction. It had done that several times, and she didn't understand why it happened.

They took turns, with small numbers of students hiding while the others tracked them.

The internal wards had been reinforced in the classroom, a few nearby rooms, and a small section of the hallways for the exercise to force the students to employ the advanced tracking technique. Her target was Sara, and she had personally seen her friend pluck the hair. She should have been able to find her with ease.

Briefly, she wondered if she used some sort of illusion or invisibility spell. The kitsune might be weak at such types of magic, but that didn't mean she couldn't use them.

The needle reversed several times over the next few minutes of her search. The next time it happened, she closed her eyes and cast a quick flare spell.

"Ow!" someone said from behind her and something thudded against the door.

Raine spun. "Got you, Sara."

It was Evie, though, who had also been seeking, not hiding. She rubbed her dilated eyes. Her glass lay on its side, its contents splashed over the floor.

Raine sighed. "Sorry. I thought Sara was invisible and right behind me." She looked to her side and realized that they now stood in front of their original classroom.

Professor Hudson stood in the doorway, her lips pursed and her brow furrowed. "This is unusual. You're not the only one having trouble. It's very rare that every student has so much difficulty. Raine, what's your particular issue?"

"The needle constantly flips back and forth, like Sara's invisible and is running around me."

The professor sighed and stepped into the classroom. She crooked her finger.

Sara stepped to the front of the class and waved, a huge grin on her face.

"Where does your needle point now?" Professor Hudson asked.

Raine looked at her glass. "Directly at me."

Evie cast a quick spell to dry the spill before she retrieved her empty glass. "Mine constantly spun like crazy."

The professor frowned. "I see."

A few other frustrated students walked down the hallway. They glared at their glasses and muttered under their breath.

"I suppose we'll have to restart and try again." The professor sighed and shook her head. "How peculiar. I don't think I've ever seen an entire class unable to cast this spell after days of practice before."

CHAPTER TWENTY-FOUR

Raine stared at the small handwritten note, her jaw tight. She stood in the hallway near the potions classroom along with William and Cameron.

Up and up I go, but I always fall back. Everyone needs me, and I'm the first thing they see. Or am I the second thing they see? Better find me before lunch, or someone will get coated.

It was day one of the Second Annual Trickster Prank War, and someone had slipped the note under Raine's dorm room door shortly before class. She had met briefly with William and Cameron to talk about it throughout the day whenever they could, but they now had less than fifteen minutes before lunch and were no closer to solving the riddle.

She sighed. "It's harder than I thought to try to stop pranks when you still have to go to class. In comparison, the 1st will almost be easier."

William rubbed his chin. "It's hard to apply FBI investigation techniques on such a tight timeline."

Cameron growled his annoyance. "It's like a ticking bomb."

"But it looks like they've not gone crazy on the first day, I mean they have one prank for half the day. We can work with that. It means they're focusing on quality over quantity."

The shifter nodded. "It also means that they've put their entire team together to try to set some of these things up. The magic involved could be a lot more complicated if that's the case."

Raine shook the note. "But I don't understand what the riddle means. It has something to do with air magic, but I have no idea where they might be doing the magic."

William thought through their possible options. "What if we tracked them?"

"That would be seven people if we count Sara." She sighed. "And they might not be near where the prank will actually happen. They might even count on us to try that and purposefully spread themselves around to lead us away from the real site. And I don't trust my tracking magic right now."

"It wasn't only you, Raine. Even Professor Hudson's confused about what happened. Don't worry about it."

"Forget tracking," Cameron said. "They won't cheat straight up, even if they mess with us a little. They have too much pride to do that, which means the key is in the clue they gave us. What goes up and up and always falls back?"

The half-Ifrit shrugged. "Dorvu?"

Raine shook her head. "He doesn't really fall when he comes down."

"Things you throw."

She tilted her head as she thought that over. "Because of gravity."

William nodded. "Yes. Unless someone uses magic, gravity is still important."

"Something that goes up and up but is pulled down by gravity." Raine half-closed her eyes as she tried to narrow the possibilities. "There are so many different things, but who are they, and what is the first thing they see?"

"Light?"

Cameron shrugged. "A doctor or a midwife?"

"That doesn't really make sense." Her eyes widened. "The students here. That's who they're talking about. What's the first real thing the students here see?"

William worked his jaw for a few seconds and sighed. "The roof of their dorm room when they wake up?"

Raine shook her head. "If we're specific, it's probably the gates and then the woods, but there's only one first thing they see that contains something going up and coming down. You could possibly argue that it's the first real thing they see."

"The circle-drive fountain," they shouted in unison.

The trio raced down the hallway and separated only to avoid bowling a confused-looking freshman over. They sprinted all the way to the front of the foyer and past the grand staircase and rushed outside to the circle drive.

A dozen students stood and chatted in the area, but none of the Tricksters were present.

Raine, William, and Cameron headed directly to the fountain.

"There has to be some way to disarm the bomb," the shifter said.

A nearby student squeaked in alarm. "Bomb?"

"It's only a prank. Don't worry about it." He frowned. "But stay away from the fountain if you don't want to end up covered in chicken feathers or something."

Raine drew her wand as she tried to decide what she should do. There was too much magic around the fountain area to simply focus on that, but the nature of the prank war meant there also had to be some way to disarm it. Maybe finding it would automatically do that.

She cast a hasty revelation spell on a section of the fountain, but nothing happened. Everything she'd learned about the magic indicated that it was rather area specific.

"You start on the opposite side, and let's circle and use revelation magic." Her heart pounded. "Cameron, keep a look out for any Tricksters. It also might be an ambush."

Her companions nodded.

She and William circled the fountain and cast their spells. A larger crowd began to gather and watched them with a mixture of befuddlement and amusement. After a few minutes, her latest attempt revealed glowing writing on the edge of the fountain. The same writing appeared on the opposite side.

We didn't say whose lunch. Not everyone has the same lunch. If you want to stop the prank, a person must be touching the timer on each side when it hits 00:00. Hope you brought a spare.

A glowing timer ticked down. There was only a couple of minutes left.

Raine slapped her hand on the timer on her side. William mirrored her action.

"We've got this," she said with a triumphant grin. "It was

close, but we got this."

Cameron grimaced and shook his head. "No. There's another prank."

"Huh? What do you mean?"

"The clue also mentioned the second thing the students see."

She groaned. "Meaning what?"

He pointed toward the mansion. "The grand stairs."

William muttered a curse under his breath and shook his head. "What if we need two people there, too?"

"It can't be like that," she said. "They know we only have three people on our team."

Cameron jogged toward the mansion. "Maybe they want us to recruit someone to help." He increased speed and rushed toward the doors, threw them open, and barreled inside.

Raine looked at her hand that half-covered the countdown. "What if we're wrong? What if this is a decoy?"

William glanced quickly from the fountain to the building. "The stairs might be the decoy, too."

"The fancy double-countdown might be to misdirect us."

"It all depends on what the Tricksters think is fair."

She groaned. "So we have to depend on the fairness of a wannabe secret society dedicated to pranks and tricks? I'm starting to think we didn't think this through all that well."

He laughed. "We'll probably end up covered in slime or feathers or something worse if we're wrong."

The crowd around them had thickened even more and students murmured amongst themselves. If some massive mess spell erupted, dozens of students might be affected.

From what they had seen of the Tricksters last year, that wasn't really their style, but they might have decided to go crazier with the idea that Team FBI would be blamed if things got out of hand.

Raine stared at the countdown. Thirty seconds. Twenty-five.

She swallowed. "I should have cast a shield spell before I put my hand down. I'm too afraid to lift it now."

"We, who are about to be slimed, salute you." William grinned.

Fifteen. Ten. Five. Four. Three. Two. One.

The writing disappeared, and an image of the FBI seal with a huge +1 appeared above the fountain for a few seconds before it vanished.

The two friends laughed. They gave each other exuberant high-fives.

"We did it," Raine shouted. "Go Team FBI!"

Several nearby students eyed them with confusion before a ripple of whispers and gasps spread from the back of the crowd. The students parted to reveal Cameron who had been splattered head-to-toe with sticky rainbow scales.

The shifter snorted. "It turns out that you needed two people inside, too, but the spell only worked on me."

"Probably because you touched it." She gave him an apologetic smile.

"Everyone else around me was too afraid to put their hand on the counter."

He growled, and his eyes flashed yellow. "I need a shower."

It was now a tie. Team Trickster one and Team FBI one.

CHAPTER TWENTY-FIVE

The last day of the war loomed, the ultimate day for the Live Unnecessary Tricksters—April Fool's Day. The battles in the preceding days had gone both ways, even if the professors did make it clear that they wanted the war over with sooner rather than later. Raine was actually surprised how much they tolerated considering some of the Tricksters' pranks.

From aural unpleasantness in the gym to Sara's failed prank—an effort to convince Raine that the Veil had parted and angry spirits had come out—the two teams had continued to battle it out. Only an hour remained until 5:00 PM, and the score remained tied at Team Trickster, eleven, and Team FBI, eleven. The next prank would decide the victors.

Some of the clues in the preceding days had been less like riddles and more general warnings. The net result was hours of paranoia, some of which protected Team FBI and some of which sent them to their doom as they over-thought the meaning of the clues.

The trio now stood in front of the circle drive fountain and searched for any Tricksters. They hadn't received another clue since they'd managed to prevent the last prank an hour earlier. For the last fifteen minutes, they had watched from the fountain.

A freshman girl wandered toward Raine, a confused look on her face. "Hey, Raine, I know we don't really know each other, but someone asked me to give this to you." She held an envelope up.

"Thanks." Raine drew a deep breath and took it.

The girl scurried off and glanced over her shoulder every few yards as if the team might curse her when she wasn't looking.

Raine opened the envelope and extracted a small black piece of paper.

A drawing of a mouth appeared on it, which immediately began to speak, the voice modulated and distorted. "The final battle now comes, and you'll have to decide how much you'll risk. The hidden witch, the son of fire, and the wolf are three who are one, but can they protect the four who are one? Remember the weather." The paper burst into flame, and she released it.

She nibbled her lip. "They're really into this. I'm not even sure if this is a prank war anymore versus some weird riddle challenge."

"Yeah, sure." Cameron grunted. "You haven't been covered with peanut butter, scales, or whatever that weird-smelling mist was. It's a prank war." He grimaced. "I can still smell it in my nostrils."

William raised his hand. A flame appeared, and his grin looked evil. "We'll show them. I still owe them for what they did to my hair. I'm lucky Evie happened to have a potion to fix it." He patted his head. "And I'm still trying to convince people that it wasn't me making that smell the other day. Now, half the school whispers behind my back and calls me Sulfur Butt," he grumbled.

"Sorry." Raine gave him an apologetic look. She took a deep breath and released it slowly. "We have to decipher the clue. The four who are one? Four people? Four friends?"

The shifter looked perplexed. "Do you think they're talking about Adrien, Philip, Evie, and Christie?"

"Philip's in town, and I don't think the Tricksters would risk involving him in town, especially when he's doing volunteer work."

William shook his head. "Not everything's about targeting a person. Remember your dorm room door?"

She sighed. "Ugh. I have to thank Christie and Evie again for cleaning that up."

"What's the plan, then?" Cameron asked. "Go to our dorm rooms and look around again?"

"No. I don't think they would choose the same place twice. Maybe it has nothing to do with those four. They haven't targeted them at all before, and it doesn't seem like Trickster style to involve them when they know they explicitly didn't want to be part of it." She nodded, satisfied with that conclusion. "We might not have time for full FBI forensics, but we can apply another technique."

"What?"

"Profiling." Raine raised a finger. "We know the Tricksters, despite what they say, are more into self-perceived challenges than pranks for the sake of pranks. This isn't order versus chaos. This is a battle of wits. Their first prank war was mainly focused among themselves and Sara. And this one has been focused on us."

Cameron shrugged. "Maybe they realize that's the only way the professors will let them get away with it. If they start sliming, stinking up, and balding half the school, the headmistress would shut them down in a second."

"The reasons don't really matter as much as the fact that they limit themselves. So, we should assume they will not target random students. If the four who are one aren't the rest of the FBI Trouble Squad, then the clue must mean something else and not another set of students in the dorm."

She gestured to the cloudless sky. "And what was that clue about the weather? It's been clear for the last few days. They had no reason to expect a storm."

"Four that become one. Storm." Cameron's nostril flared.

His companions looked at him and he chuckled.

"You don't get it because you're not a shifter."

"What?" Raine asked.

"When I shift, I become four-legged." He patted his leg. "Four legs become one animal."

"Do you think they're going after another shifter? Or you?"

He shook his head. "The weather."

Still confused, she looked at the sky and shrugged.

"You might have not been able to ride him much this year, but Storm's still your favorite horse."

Raine gasped. "They wouldn't do something to Storm, would they?"

William scoffed. "Maybe not him, but maybe his stable. Let's go."

———

Storm munched contentedly on fresh hay but looked up when they arrived. He was fine and happy to see Raine. She scratched and petted him for a few minutes while William searched the surrounding stall and stable for any hidden messages or spells. He couldn't find anything.

She frowned as they stepped out of the stable. "Maybe it's a trick in the end, or we've misunderstood what they meant."

William shook his head. "No, I think Cameron's right. This has something to do with Storm."

The shifter threw his arm up to stop her from advancing. "Yes. It had to do with using Storm as bait." His eyes flashed yellow and he narrowed them as he pointed downward.

Her gaze followed his direction and she frowned. A thin white line stretched across the path and hovered about a half an inch off the ground. "A good old-fashioned tripwire? Except magical?"

William scowled. "Why not simply make it invisible?"

"Because this is a prank war, not a real war." She gestured toward the stable. "You guys get back in there. I'll try to trip it with a spell, but I want you both safe. You're right. I'm the only member of Team FBI who hasn't suffered yet. It's my turn."

Cameron shook his head. "I can do it."

"No." Raine gave him her best stubborn face. "This is

the final battle in the war, and it's time I put my non-sticky and nice-smelling hair on the line, too." She shook her head. "I liked Sara's prank better. It was more about tricking someone than merely being gross."

William gave her a salute and jogged toward the building.

The shifter finally nodded. "Be careful. They might have something disgusting we haven't even thought of." He walked slowly away but glanced at her a few times.

She backed away from the tripwire and checked her surroundings cautiously to make sure she wouldn't head right into another one. Once she was ten yards away, she raised her wand and took a deep breath. The prank war was about to be decided.

Poised and ready, she hesitated for a moment and wondered if she should try to dispel the tripwire or cut it. After a few seconds, she decided on a simpler cutting spell.

The wire snapped, and a cloud of pink particles puffed dramatically from where it had been. She retreated hastily as the pink cloud drifted and descended slowly, and the particles sizzled as they touched the grass before they vanished. An FBI seal appeared a moment later alongside a +2.

Raine waved at the stable, grateful Horace wasn't there. He would have been irate, even if the magic didn't seem to have affected the grass. The spell must have been designed to only interact with the members of Team FBI. She didn't really care about the particulars as they didn't matter. Her team had won.

Something moved on the stable roof. She frowned and

squinted and finally identified an elf with long gray hair. Jillian.

The Gray Elf somersaulted off and displayed the preternatural reflexes of her race. She sprinted toward Raine, her normally calm expression twisted in fear and her eyes wide.

"Raine, get out of there!" she yelled.

Cameron rushed out of the stable and toward Raine, but he was already a good ten yards behind Jillian.

"What?" Raine blinked.

The air hissed behind her and she spun instinctively. The pink particles had ceased to sizzle and disappear and now floated upward.

A few rocketed toward her and exploded. She cried out in pain and lost her wand as she fell a few feet away.

The elf closed the distance and threw herself on top of the witch as she hastily cast a shield spell. The pink cloud transformed into a deadly magical Roman candle that spewed a kaleidoscopic rainbow of deadly exploding balls. Jillian wrapped herself around Raine and gasped in pain as the magical orbs struck and her shield strained. By the time Cameron arrived, the attack was over.

The Trickster lay on top of Raine, her breathing shallow, holes seared through her clothes, and her body covered in burns. Her shields hadn't held. Raine only had a single shallow burn on her hand.

"Sorry, Raine," the elf whispered. "I cheated. I left the figurine in my dorm room so I could see how things would turn out. I wasn't...going to change anything, and then I saw...something go wrong. I don't...even know..." Her head slumped forward, and she passed out.

CHAPTER TWENTY-SIX

Raine rubbed her wrists as she waited in Headmistress Berens' office with William and Cameron. The shifter had immediately carried Jillian to the nurse, who sent all three to the office to report the incident.

Once the headmistress heard what had happened, she told them to wait in her office while she personally checked on the elf. The three stood there in silence as the minutes stretched on and reflected on how a fun prank war had ended with a girl badly burned and almost killed.

After a while, Raine couldn't take the silence anymore.

"What was that even about?" she muttered and shook her head. "That wasn't a prank. That could have killed me, and it wasn't like anything else they tried during the entire war."

Cameron growled, still stressed and shaken by what had happened. "I don't know what happened, but Jillian didn't seem to expect it. I think we're lucky she didn't use her figurine and had the vision. If the full force of that spell had hit you, it wouldn't be a matter of it *could* have killed you. It *would* have killed you. You saw how badly she was wounded, and she at least managed to summon a shield from what I could see."

Raine nodded. "It happened so quickly, but she did cast a shield spell right before she covered me. It's like she was only worried about making sure I didn't get hurt." She looked at her hand. The nurse had healed her minor burn from the incident. "I didn't even have time to think. The whole thing barely registered in my mind."

William curled his hands into fists. "If this was some stupid, dangerous prank that went wrong, I'll never forgive them. That was way over the line."

She shook her head. "Jillian nearly died, and her first thought was to save me. If she'd planned something like this, she wouldn't have rushed over like that. She would have known what to expect and anyway, the Tricksters aren't like that."

"I don't know about that. I don't know if I trust—"

The door opened, and Headmistress Berens stepped inside, her expression tense. She didn't say anything as she walked around the students and settled behind her desk.

"The first thing I want you to know is that Jillian's okay," she related after a short silence. "She's been healed, but she's tired from everything that happened. I've already talked to her about what occurred. I wanted to get information as soon as possible, as it's not all that often that one of my students almost dies from what's supposed to be a harmless prank."

"Was that spell her fault?" William asked with a grim frown.

The headmistress shook her head but looked concerned, nevertheless. "From what she tells me, the final spell was supposed to cover whoever tripped it with chocolate, vanilla, and strawberry syrup. They had set it up to only activate if a magical tripped it."

Raine rubbed her wrists once more. "Did I mess it up when I cut it?"

"No. The way the spell was configured, if anything, it should have launched the dessert coatings when you did that, rather than turning into a deadly magical artillery barrage. The underlying spells are completely different in their nature." The headmistress' mouth squeezed into a tight line for a few seconds. "The only word I can think of to describe it is bizarre."

"Bizarre?"

"Yes. I sent Professor Powell to check near the stable, and he informed me that the magical signature there was odd. The magic did seem to originate from what we would expect from Gray Elf magic, but it was slightly warped compared to normal residue."

"Could it have been something like some of the misfires Sara had when she was still learning to control her magic?" Raine asked. "She had more than a few weird things happen before her magic fully came in."

Headmistress Berens didn't respond for a moment. "I recall all that, but that's also unlikely. Kitsune magic has a particular nature that makes it more...dynamic, you could say. Gray Elf magic isn't like that, and Jillian came to this school with her full magical potential already available. Even then, the nature of the misfire was so antithetical to what the intent was, it raises a number of questions and concerns about what actually happened."

"Meaning what?" Cameron asked. "Was it some sort of attack?"

"All the evidence we have does suggest that Jillian set the spell up. The point of confusion remains solely why it misfired in such a dramatic and unexpected manner. Given how apologetic the girl is, I doubt her intention was anything so dangerous. Despite their pretensions to stealth, I've been well aware of each of these Tricksters since they started here, and their predilections do not include harmful stunts. Otherwise, they would have been expelled a long time ago. That said, however, I'm relieved that your little prank competition is over." The headmistress shook her head. "There are still a number of questions that remain unanswered about what happened. This isn't the only odd incident as of late, but magic is almost a living force at times—as you're well aware of from the Arc Eighty-Eight incident."

Raine bit her lip and nodded. "What should we do? Is there anything we can do?"

"For now? Nothing. I wouldn't advise any more complicated magical competitions or spells without staff supervision. We're only fortunate that Jillian wasn't killed." Headmistress Berens frowned. "And until the staff has a better understanding of what happened, the last thing we need is students trying to handle a dangerous situation, even the FBI Trouble Squad."

Her cheeks heated. "I'm sorry. We never intended for anything like this to happen. It was only supposed to be a fun little game. Team Trickster versus Team FBI."

"You misunderstand my intent. I don't blame you, and this isn't your fault, Raine. You didn't set the spell up. Jillian did, and she was the main person injured in this incident." She looked firmly at the three students as if to emphasize her next statement. "You have to understand that the spell that resulted isn't even something she is capable of. Yes, people can exceed their magical capabilities, but that only tends to happen during active casting, not with a passive, complicated spell set up like she had done for your little competition."

Raine swallowed and her stomach tightened. "Do you think this could have anything to do with Maeve and Arc Eighty-Eight? Could she have escaped?"

"No, Maeve no longer exists in this world, and if it was her, we'd know. Professor Powell made it clear that the magic does seem to be related to Gray Elves in nature—or at least it doesn't feel anything like the magic associated with the Arc Eighty-Eight incident. There's only so much a magical being can do to fundamentally hide the nature of its imprint on the world when it uses magic, especially one as unusual as Maeve was."

William frowned. "Wait. You had him check for all that already? You expected it?"

"Of course I had him check, and no, I didn't expect it. When certain high-profile incidents occur and other strange things subsequently happen, the most intelligent course of action is to investigate for similar links. This obviously had nothing to do with Noel Tucker's secret society, so going back to the Arc Eighty-Eight incident was a logical choice." Headmistress Berens narrowed her eyes and stared at her desk, perhaps to consider information she wasn't eager to share with the students.

Raine could only guess at the burden a woman like the school head might carry.

Finally, she forced a smile. "For now, it doesn't help us to speculate. Jillian's fine, and the staff will look into the incident. You should all concentrate on your classes and extracurricular activities, and I'm impressed with how you didn't panic and immediately brought her to the nurse. You may very well have saved her life."

Raine shook her head. "Jillian saved my life first. All we did was return the favor."

CHAPTER TWENTY-SEVEN

Sara marched back and forth in the dorm room, her face almost as red as her hair and her arms folded. Every once in a while, her fingers twitched. "If she hadn't almost already died, I would strangle her. I can't believe this happened. This is what I get for letting those Tricksters spin me up with all this prank stuff."

Raine sighed as she lay atop her covers. "Jillian didn't mean to do it. Even Headmistress Berens doesn't know what happened. There's no point in getting angry about it. I'm sure Jillian feels terrible."

"I'll no longer do anything with them." The kitsune shook her head. "I didn't like a lot of their pranks anyway. They're too into gross stuff. Kitsune magic is supposed to be playful trickster magic, not covering a shifter with sticky scales magic."

"Again, it's not her fault. Her magic backfired or misfired, or something." Raine shrugged. "And she threw herself in front of the spell to save me. That has to mean something."

She was glad Evie and Christie were still out in town. It was hard enough to handle her friend right now without the others present.

Sara stopped her angry marching and took a deep breath. "Okay, I'll give her credit for that, even though every part of me wants to be angry with her." She rubbed her temples. "What were we thinking to get involved in a prank war anyway, especially one that lasted over several days?" She flopped onto her bed and groaned. "With our luck, Rhazdon, Genghis Khan, and the Council will invade the Spring Formal and force us all to dance disco."

Raine rolled onto her side. "That would be impressive, actually. Funny, too."

"You know why I'm really so bothered?" The girl sat and rested her hands in her lap.

"Why?"

"I was already half-worried about something crazy like that happening, and I thought it would be my fault. Just because my magic's fully in doesn't mean it's not trickster magic. Even though I can cast normal spells, too, a lot of what I do is to simply use my energy and see what happens. I didn't want my prank to depend too much on really specific magic for that reason. I didn't want someone to be hurt because I was careless." She held her hand up. "Before you say anything, I get it. It wasn't Jillian's fault, but I still can't help but want to blame her for you almost getting hurt. Stupid pranks."

She nodded. "I thought your prank was the best, by the way. At least in idea. If it was closer to Halloween, I might have bought it more, but no one ever talks about Veil spirits coming to the campus in April." She shrugged. "I might have even bought it if you had Madelyn around and could blame it on her condition."

The kitsune made a face. "There's no way I would involve Madelyn in a prank. The poor girl would have a stroke."

"Probably. I've talked to her more this semester, but it's hard to get her to open up."

"Not everyone will, but I do feel sorry for her, especially with the way her sister bosses her around."

She shrugged. "Vianna only wants what's best for her, I think."

"Maybe."

Someone knocked on the door and Raine pushed up to answer it.

Jillian stood on the other side, a small colorful paper bag in hand. "May I come in?"

Raine gestured inside. She didn't return to her bed. Instead, she sat in her desk chair. "Are you feeling okay?"

"That's a loaded question." The elf shrugged. She walked over to Raine and offered her the bag. "That's some candy I bought in the kemana the last time I went. It's not much, but it's at least the beginning of me saying I'm sorry."

She took the bag and set it on the desk. "That's not necessary. I know that you didn't try to hurt me. We talked to the headmistress about it, and you did save my life."

Jillian scoffed. "I lucked into that only because I wanted to cheat a little, and I almost didn't. If I hadn't had the premonition or kept using the figurine, you would have—" She hissed and turned away. "You have to understand, Raine. Harming people goes against what it means to be a

Live Unnecessary Trickster. Pranks are supposed to be about challenging others and exposing the absurdities of the world. That kind of thing. Not being mean and hurting people. I asked Kenneth if he wanted to kick me out and he said he doesn't want to, but I'll quit if you want me to. I owe you that much."

"You don't have to quit your group, Jillian. Mistakes happen, especially with magic. The important thing is that everyone is okay. The staff is looking into it to find out what happened. You don't have to beat yourself up over it."

Sara muttered something under her breath, but Raine was sure it was, "Yes, let me beat you up over it."

The elf's gray-eyed gaze locked on Raine's face for a long moment before it flicked to the frowning kitsune. "And I'll apologize to you as well, Sara. We involved your friend in our competition, and she was almost hurt because of it."

The other girl snorted.

Raine sent her a pleading look. "I wanted to be involved. Sara didn't drag me in against my will, and yes, it ended weirdly and dangerously, but I had fun until then." She managed a quiet laugh. "I didn't get hit by any of the pranks. So maybe all the good luck had to be balanced out by bad luck."

Jillian took a few deep breaths and nodded. "Oh, you should also know that as far as the Live Unnecessary Tricksters are concerned, Team FBI clearly won the prank war."

Sara frowned. "Seriously? You're talking about that now?"

Raine shook her head at the kitsune, who rolled her eyes and looked away.

"Thanks," Raine said. "Even if I'm not into pranks like you guys, I know how much this all means to you, and I want you to understand that I don't blame you for what happened."

The girl gave a shallow nod, her eyes downcast. "I should get going."

Sara sighed and stood. "I might be angry about what happened, but you did literally throw yourself in the line of fire to save one of my best friends, so I'm grateful for that."

Jillian shook her head. "I only wish I knew why that happened." She stepped outside and closed the door.

Raine sighed. "Well, that's over, at least. I think we should be able to get ready for the Spring Formal without anyone being mortally wounded."

CHAPTER TWENTY-EIGHT

Raine felt strange looking through racks of dresses in a Charlottesville's department store after everything that had happened the day before. She had considered not going, but Sara—of all people—insisted and firmly declared that it would be good to move on.

Cameron also told her to go. He argued that Jillian would feel worse if she stopped doing the things she would have done because of what had happened. The headmistress hadn't restricted anyone's movements either, and they were almost out of time before the dance. Everyone wanted to go dress shopping together, and the prank war had ended up distracting her. She had to go for her friends' sakes as well.

Sara, Raine, Evie, and Christie's choice of a Charlottesville shopping trip over Ruby Falls was motivated by something Raine couldn't have predicted.

Evie draped two dresses over her arm. "The theme of the Spring Formal is still weird, I think."

Sara glanced around to make sure no one else was

nearby. "It's actually straight-forward. Glamor in the mundane."

"That's code for 'no magical dresses.'"

"It makes things easier. Sometimes, you simply want to wear clothes."

Christie draped her seventh dress over her arm. The combined fabric almost looked like it weighed more than the girl.

"I went to talk to the Student Council about it," she began, "and they said they were concerned that some students were overwhelmed by all the complicated themes, so they thought to themselves, 'How do we make this easier?' And one way to make it easier was to make it a normal dance, so that's what they decided on." She nodded and took a deep breath.

Sara scoffed. "I think this proves that not having Philip and Raine on the Student Council leads to them having trouble coming up with good ideas."

Raine chose a blue dress off the rack. "I don't think that's it. I think what they told Christie is the truth. We all know we've struggled with some of the themes, and it's already hard enough to pick the right dress without worrying about whether it has other cool features." She tapped her lips in thought before she selected a red dress as well. It wouldn't hurt to try it on.

Unlike the others, Sara didn't have multiple garments. She'd homed in on an emerald-green dress after being in the store for only two minutes.

"I think it's good to do something fun and relaxing." Evie peered at a dark-purple creation but didn't add it to her stack. "Everyone's so stressed about everything. Classes, the championship, the prank stuff."

Christie nodded. "Adrien thinks he's relaxed, but his idea of that is only to push himself one hundred and five percent instead of one hundred and ten percent. I constantly tell him he doesn't have to carry everything on his own shoulders, but he always rattles off the duties of the captain. It's attractive and boring at the same time. How does that work?"

Raine smiled. "That's Adrien, I guess. I think he would have—" Her breath caught, and she glanced hastily at the other students. "Do you feel that?" she whispered.

They all nodded, obviously disturbed by the massive pulse of magic. The last time she had felt that much magic was during the Arc Eighty-Eight incident.

A woman with bright pink hair and oversized sunglasses stepped into the store, her loose floral summer dress a little thin given how cool the temperatures remained in the area. Her black combat boots didn't seem to go with the outfit, but her macramé tote did. Raine was no expert on fashion, but she thought the customer had made a good choice to buy new outfits.

Despite the fact she was across the store, she marched directly toward them and ignored several other people along the way.

Raine didn't recognize her at all. She hung her dresses on the rack and slid a hand surreptitiously toward her wand inside her coat pocket. For all they knew, the woman was a Raven Clan assassin who had been sent to kill anyone who was friends with Adrien.

The other girls also set their dresses down and tension lined their faces.

The woman slowed and gave them a double thumbs-up. "You shouldn't go there."

Raine blinked. "Go where?"

"That school, of course." The woman rolled her eyes. "Incorrect. That's what it is. I followed you. Oh, I know where the jitney goes. I saw you trying to be normal. Boring. Why? Because the school makes you. They can ask, and you can tell them to screw off."

It seemed pointless to deny that they went to the school. Given the magic they sensed from the woman, she was a powerful witch.

Raine's heart rate kicked up. There was one powerful witch who was possibly supposed to come into the area. The woman didn't match the description she'd last seen for Eris, but the Queen Witch of Chaos was known to change her appearance constantly. Apparently, to look the same from day to day was boring and not chaotic enough. It was only her tendency to not lie about who she was that allowed witnesses to point the government at her.

"What's incorrect about the school, Eris?" she asked, her eyes narrowed.

"You know who I am?" She clapped. "How adorable."

Evie paled and Raine took a deep breath.

"As for the school," Eris continued. "It's wrong. Closed-minded. Small. You know it. They keep you locked up and tell you not to talk about it because people might be afraid." She tittered. "Anyone who's afraid of the truth is a fool. They should be scared. They should be uncomfortable." She pointed a pale finger at Raine. "Are you scared?"

She squared her shoulders and lowered her hand away from her wand. Any attempt to duel with the witch in a department store would only end with her defeat and innocent people hurt, but she refused to show any fear. That wasn't what an FBI trainee should do. "Scared of what? You?"

"Why would you be scared of me?" Eris lowered her glasses for a moment. Her eyes were a surprisingly normal brown. She raised the glasses again. "What? Will you defend the honor of your school, little girl?"

Sara frowned. "You'd better not talk badly about the school."

The woman jerked her head toward the kitsune. "Be angry. Perfect. That's great." She threw her hands in the air. "Anger can be cleansing. It stops the status quo. The status quo is death. Static. Boring."

Raine took another deep breath. Even if she didn't want to fight the witch, she needed to make her believe it would cost her if she tried something.

"I won't let you hurt anyone," she said through gritted teeth. "No matter what it takes."

Christie and Evie exchanged concerned looks. Sara's hand edged toward her pocket.

"Hurt anyone?" The woman shook her head. "I don't hurt anyone. I free people." She shook a finger at them. "I see what's happening here because I see in your eyes that you know. Are they talking about me?"

Evie paled and swallowed. "Maybe we should go."

Christie looked from Raine to the woman and took a breath. "I don't appreciate you bashing the school, but I don't even know who you are. I actually like the crazy style you have going, but then again, the whole anti-school attitude counts against it."

Eris' expression turned feral. "True beauty."

"Excuse me?"

"I'll show you all true beauty." The woman flicked her wrist. "I can see it. Taste it. Smell it. The hatred. The fear. They have sown that in you because they're cowards. Do you trust them? Their kind lied for thousands of years. Static. Order. Unchanging. Death."

Evie cleared her throat. "Excuse me, ma'am. We simply want to buy dresses here."

The witch took a few steps back, her movement serpentine. "I'm not what you think, little girls."

"Then what are you?" Raine asked.

"I'm freedom. You've seen it already." She bowed with a dramatic flourish. "I'm sure you've seen it at the school already even if you don't want to recognize it."

"I have no idea what you're talking about."

Sara frowned. "If you don't leave us alone, we'll have to call the authorities."

Raine tried to keep a stern look on her face but inside, she worried. She wasn't sure if Sara was bluffing.

Eris giggled. "Oh, you're a fiery one." She ran her tongue along her bottom lip. "You're not ready yet. I guess you need to be...marinated more." She winked and continued to back away.

"You've made a big mistake," Raine said quietly and shook her head.

"Why? Oh. Because you'll tell? It doesn't matter. None of you will see it coming. Freedom is painful to those who have never known it. Such people always try to reject it." Eris slid a hand into her tote and removed her wand.

Raine's eyes widened. "Don't. Please. I'm begging you. There are innocent people in this store."

"Don't? Innocent people? Those boring people at the school have poisoned your mind, little girl." The witch laughed and returned her wand to her purse. "You'll taste freedom and true beauty soon enough. Until then, toodles!" She turned and skipped toward the entrance.

"We should buy our dresses today," Raine said. "Because I'm reasonably sure we won't be allowed to leave the school for a while."

Christie looked around in real bewilderment. "Can someone please tell me what's going on?"

"That was the Witch Queen of Chaos."

"Oh." The girl made a face that reflected everyone's disquiet.

CHAPTER TWENTY-NINE

M ara sighed as the girls related their encounter. She'd hoped that Eris would bypass the area. Other than distracting Agent Oliver, the specter of the witch's presence seemed to smother the semester.

"Are you sure it was her?" she asked.

Raine shrugged. "She didn't look like her last picture, but she answered to the name Eris, and she talked like a crazy chaos witch. She really seemed to hate the school, too, which would make sense if it was her."

"That does sound like persuasive evidence." She sighed.

Of course, she would need to inform Agent Oliver, Bruce, and the staff right away, but the question remained how best to handle the situation. She did not want the PDA to turn the school into a war zone.

Raine sighed and exchanged glances with her friends. "What should we do?"

"Nothing," Mara said.

"Nothing?"

The headmistress nodded. "One thing you'll learn as

you get older is that there are always threats out there. If we always avoid living life because of them, we'll miss much joy. It was a lesson that took me far too long to remember." Raine looked confused, but Mara didn't see the need to clarify her and Xander's relationship. "You should enjoy your Spring Formal. Eris won't be able to set foot on campus without every teacher, gnome, and pixie in the school knowing. We also have the PDA in town. You students will be safe. Leave the fugitive witch to the adults."

Doubt clouded the girl's expression even as relief spread over her friends' faces. She nodded, but Mara doubted the situation would end without the FBI Trouble Squad being involved.

Less than fifteen minutes after she dismissed the students, Agent Oliver, Bruce, and Xander gathered in her office.

The PDA agent's eager smile surprised her.

"It looks like we were right at the PDA," she said. "And Eris has grown even more arrogant."

"It seems that way, but I'm still concerned. The presence of this witch and some of the timing of the strange magical…backfires, I suppose is a good word, are hard to ignore. Her statements to the students imply as much."

"Eris lies like normal people breathe," the other woman scoffed. "You worry too much. She doesn't have the ability to disrupt other people's magic like that. It's purely a coincidence."

Xander gave her a thin smile. "Are you sure?"

"Yes. Note that it's only student magic that has been

affected." Agent Oliver shrugged. "If she had developed some unusual ability to cause magical misfire, why hasn't she used it on the PDA in the past? Or any of the adults at the school?"

Mara pondered that before she nodded cautiously. "That's true. The wards are secure as well. If she had penetrated them, we would know."

"Besides," Bruce said, "she's not the kind of woman who would have been quiet about beating the wards, especially given what she told the students."

"I agree." The other agent frowned. "That said, we can't have her approaching students. I recommend you keep everyone on campus until as such time as the PDA has captured her."

Both men nodded.

"It's a reasonable precaution," Mara said. "I'll prepare the announcement right away."

CHAPTER THIRTY

R aine rested her head on Cameron's shoulder as a slow ballad played. His hands settled on her hips as they swayed to the music. She had chosen a dark-blue dress in the end, and although the restriction to the school grounds meant she couldn't have her hair done in either Ruby Falls or Charlottesville, a little magic and helpful roommates went a long way to produce a lovely updo.

"It's weird," she murmured.

"Weird?" he asked. "I think my dancing's pretty good." He winked.

"It's not you. It's me."

"I like your dancing, too."

She raised her head and nodded. "I feel so relaxed."

"You're supposed to have a good time at dances." He grinned. "And a good time with me. Why wouldn't you feel relaxed?"

"Because she's out there." Raine sighed. "She came right up to us, and she was even ready to do magic. Something serious could have happened."

The shifter scoffed. "So? You heard the announcement from the headmistress. We can't leave campus for a few days, but it's not like she'll come here. And if she does, she'll have the entire staff on her. The PDA already had a number of agents in the kemana before we even count Agent Oliver." He shrugged. "Eris might normally be this big spooky chaos witch, but if she was dumb enough to harass random students buying dresses, she's too arrogant to avoid capture. I bet they have her cornered right now."

"That makes sense, but I don't know if I believe it. I want to believe it, but it feels too easy."

"You don't need to worry about it, Raine. Like I said, the professors and the PDA will take care of her." Cameron's eyes flashed yellow. "And I won't let that woman ruin our Spring Formal. If she shows up, I'll show her the power of a shifter."

Raine smiled. "You know what? You're right. This isn't like so many of the things that happened before. This woman hasn't targeted our friends, and the authorities have taken her seriously. I don't have to worry about her. There's nothing I can do that the PDA can't."

He relaxed. "That's what I want to hear. You're not Agent Raine Campbell yet. You're still a student, and it won't destroy you to enjoy that for a little longer."

She replied with a shallow nod before she looked around. All her friends were present, and everyone looked happy and relaxed. They'd worked hard that semester, and in some cases, hadn't spent as much time together as she would have liked. Some of that was the natural result of the responsibilities of junior year, and some of that was because of what Cameron had described.

Once again, she was too busy thinking of herself as Agent Raine Campbell already. Cases and criminals filled her thoughts more often than dresses, dances, and fun.

Her junior year was almost finished. It had been another blur of the fantastic and magical, but she always looked forward and focused on her FBI future.

Raine smiled softly despite a slight pang in her heart. She knew she would make things work with Cameron and stay in contact with her friends. But, once next year was over, she wouldn't be able to spend hours each day in the library. She wouldn't get to laugh when the poppy on Librarian Decker's bowler blew a raspberry or ask any of the gnomes for advice on a book. Worse, she wouldn't wake up to three great friends and be more worried about a spells test than anything else.

It wasn't merely that she would join the bureau. The reality was more than that. She would be an adult with adult responsibilities. Right there, at that dance, she could cling to her boyfriend and let the music thrum through her because of all the adults shielding them, from the professors to the PDA to Agent Connor. When Maeve took her and her friends to the strange pocket reality, even the pixies had been involved in saving them. Librarian Decker had helped them more than once.

Was that what it meant to be an adult? To protect younger people?

Raine sighed. "I'll miss this place a lot more than I realized."

Cameron frowned a little. "What place?"

"The school."

"But we're not even done with the semester."

They halted as the music stopped playing. Another song started a moment later.

He smiled at her. "Let's get something to drink."

"Okay."

Cameron led her to a table near the punch bowls and pulled out a chair for her. He headed over to grab two glasses of punch and chuckled. "After so many dances with magical themes and magical clothes and effects, having a normal one is odd." He nodded to where Adrien and Christie danced a little farther away. "That's the real magic, though."

Raine picked her drink up and took a sip of the sweet beverage. "I think I've taken this place for granted, and some of the stuff with Eris has made me realize that. I'm glad we'll go on that summer trip. It'll help the experience last that much longer."

"That won't be here, though. It'll be on an island in Maine."

"Sure, but we'll still have professors and that school atmosphere. We'll still be students, and I'll be forced to spend a couple of months not obsessing over FBI training."

Cameron frowned. "Have you heard anything about who else is going?"

"I know one of the other students is Juniper. When I last talked to Headmistress Berens, they were still deciding on the last choice, but it looked like it would be Malcolm."

"They're both okay." He shrugged.

"I think they're both nice," Raine said. "Although we'll need to be careful to include them. I'm sure it'll be weird for them to be on a trip for two months with seven other best friends, most of whom are dating one another." She laughed. "How did we end up the FBI Trouble Squad instead of something like the Sensational Seven?"

He made a face. "I think I prefer the FBI Trouble Squad."

"I'm just saying." She exhaled a contented sigh when she saw William and Evie dancing in the crowd. "Did you ever think you would make friends like this when you came here?"

The shifter looked thoughtful. "I came to this school expecting people to mess with me because I'm a shifter, and I expected that I'd have a lot of trouble." He squeezed her hand. "And I never expected to meet someone like you."

Raine entire face heated. "Likewise."

He raised a playful eyebrow. "You expected people to mess with you because you're a shifter? Is there something you're not telling me?"

She rolled her eyes. "You know what I'm saying."

"Maybe." Her boyfriend grinned and nodded to the dance floor. "Do you want to get back out there?"

"You're eager."

"It's rare that I have you all to myself, and I mean not only you being here." He tapped her chest above her heart and then her forehead. "But these, too."

"You're right." She surveyed the room and absorbed the sight all the dancing couples with a soft smile. "Tonight, I'll let the adults shoulder all the responsibility." She stood. "And I'll simply be a regular teenager."

"A regular teenage witch at a magical boarding school."

She laughed. "Sure, a regular teenager."

CHAPTER THIRTY-ONE

The crowd roared in the stands and the sound faded as the players interfaced with the Louper match. It was time to begin the semi-finals with Charlottesville Cardinals versus the Cincinnati Lions.

A dense forest of trees stretched high into the air and replaced the field and stands. The thick canopy allowed only scattered rays of light through, which gave the entire area an eerie twilight feel.

Adrien nodded to himself, satisfied. They needed to dispose of the Lions and move on to the finals.

The days of restriction to the school grounds had extended into a week, and some students began to worry that the Louper semi-final would be postponed. But, as the game didn't require the players to actually leave campus, Headmistress Berens assured everyone that the match would proceed as previously scheduled after she'd consulted with the other school and the officials who monitored the match.

The captain took a deep breath and scrutinized the

almost impenetrable foliage that filled the spaces between the massive tree trunks. "We're only two games away from being undefeated champions. We can do this. We haven't lost a match this season, so there is no reason to lose now."

The current starting lineup shouted their approval. Besides Adrien, the Cardinals players included Cody, Daniel, Hilda, and Jackson, some of their most experienced players.

Cody grinned as his tracking orb brightened. "Well, what do you know? They haven't blocked tracking. And here I thought we would have to wander around again." His grin faded almost immediately. "Oh, that's why. Well, it's one way to make it challenging."

Adrien glanced at the orb and looked up slowly. The token must be somewhere above them. They couldn't simply burst up given the way the branches connected to the tree and the non-existent space between them. It was time to climb.

"All right, let's go. The Lions have to deal with the same annoyance." He gestured to a low-hanging branch and then to another above him. "Let's do this branch to branch. Don't fall and don't try any high mobility. It's very easy to bounce off something and tumble. Remember, I can't sub you if you are taken out."

The elf took hold of the first branch and swung himself to the next. Before he moved on, he summoned a glowing rope and secured it around the tree. At every few following limbs, he repositioned the magical energy so he would only fall a limited way even if he slipped. He had confidence in his climbing skills, but he didn't want to lose the match because of arrogance.

A quick check confirmed that his team members all took similar safety precautions. The other members replicated his movements, and they scaled the tree with surprising ease.

Other than an early scare with Daniel, no one came close to falling. The branches thickened as they rose higher and higher to the point. Eventually, they could easily fit two people side by side on one of the massive branches. The botany of it didn't make sense, but Louper worlds didn't have to obey all the rules that defined true reality outside the game.

About three hundred feet up, the outline of a series of flat structures became visible with thin lines stretched between them.

The Cardinals continued to climb, and the outline resolved into wooden platforms that supported small huts and connected by rope bridges. It wasn't merely a tree house but an entire expansive village in the sky. The tracking spell had brightened and now led them through it, not to it.

Adrien nodded toward the village. "Let's be careful. If there isn't a puzzle in there, I'm sure there'll probably be monsters. Or the Lions might have set up an ambush."

The team arrived at a lower platform that provided stairs to the first main platform that formed the village. A faint buzzing sounded from above, but they hadn't seen any movement during the long process of climbing the tree. Of course, the fact that they hadn't seen anything didn't mean that they hadn't closed on their enemies.

The captain summoned a sword and cast a shield spell over himself before he jogged up the stairs. He frowned when he realized there was no obvious way in or out of any of the rude huts other than a large opening at the top— which would require someone to pull themselves out of it unless they could fly.

The structures were slapdash in construction, more collections of overlapped twigs and leaves than real construction with some kind of thick sap-like substance to bind them together.

As his team stepped onto the platform beside him, the volume of the buzzing increased. Dust puffed around the top of some of the huts as if buffeted by something inside.

Adrien hefted his sword. "Trouble's coming."

The other players assumed a wedge formation with him at the front, ready for battle.

The buzzing grew almost frantic before wasp-like men rose from the huts, their wings beating faster than could be discerned. They flew upright and their three-fingered clawed hands on two of their six legs held weapons. A dozen of the enemy emerged from the huts in total.

"Cardinals, let's do what we do best," the elf shouted. "Let's go all out."

Jackson fell to one knee. That wasn't exactly going all out, but the player looked confused.

The captain frowned. "What's going on?"

"I don't know. I can't move. It's like there's something wrong with my connection to the match. I'm trying to do what I normally do, but my avatar won't move."

It wasn't the optimal timing for a glitch. Adrien needed to move fast before the battle began.

He raised his arm to summon the substitution orb.

"Cardinals captain, substitution. This player for Marcus Park."

Once he released the orb, it hovered over Jackson and encased him in a column of light. They would have to wait two minutes before their new freshman replacement could come to the field, and they had to survive for that time hundreds of feet in the air in trees in a battle with wasp-men.

Their adversaries hadn't attacked yet, but the Cardinals hadn't stepped off the platform toward any of the huts.

"Is everyone else ready? I'll draw their attention." Adrien swung his sword a few times. He couldn't wait for the sub. Every second they spent waiting meant the Lions could gain that much more ground.

The three remaining active members of the team nodded.

"On three. One, two, three." He hurtled toward a hut.

The wasp-men broke before him and their weakness left them open to bright white magical bolts from Daniel, Cody, and Hilda. The attacks didn't pack as much punch as fireballs, but they were faster, which made it easier for the team to eliminate the flying monsters.

The elf cleaved through one of the creatures as it closed on him. He spun and stabbed another. Despite being a man down, the Cardinals defeated the winged combatants in about a minute, and no one sustained a significant hit.

Cody and Daniel both grinned.

Adrien wasn't ready to smile. "Marcus will have to catch up. Let's go."

The tracking orb guided them along the branches to a honeycomb-like structure camouflaged among a mass of dense branches.

The elf was distracted for a moment by the fact that while they had fought wasp-men in a village who lived in huts, they would now enter a honeycomb instead of a wasp's nest. He shook the thought aside impatiently and reminded himself that Louper was a fantasy battle, first and foremost.

Suddenly, Cody spun in a circle, his arms stretched to either side.

"What are you doing?" Adrien asked. "We don't have time for this."

"I'm not trying to do anything," the wizard responded. "Something's wrong."

Marcus, who had since caught up, frowned. "Is it a trap?"

Cody shook his head. "I think it's a gear problem."

The captain scrubbed a hand over his face. "We'll give it thirty seconds, and if it doesn't clear, we'll sub you out for Dennis."

The wizard continued his crazy twirls and looked more than a little ridiculous.

Adrien's jaw tightened. If their opponents, Cincinnati, didn't have these kinds of issues as well, the match might have already been lost.

He raised his arm to summon the substitution orb when his eyes widened. His teammate didn't simply spin in place. Each rotation brought him about an inch closer to the edge of the platform, and he only had a few inches left.

"Cody!" He lurched toward the senior, but it was too

late. Another rotation took him to into empty air and he plummeted.

There were no substitutions for dead players. Adrien hissed in frustration and kicked at the platform.

"Fine," he muttered. "Let's hope the Lions have also lost team members."

For the first time that season, he had to face the serious possibility that they might lose.

Small, twisted, sticky passageways filled the honeycomb structure, but no actual honey was present. Instead, a foul-smelling thick green liquid seeped from various crevasses and seemed to clog their nostrils.

The Cardinals had followed the tracking orb through the circuitous maze until they finally arrived at an irregular chamber in the center.

Fireballs and magical bolts rocketed from across the vast chamber. The four Cardinals returned fire, but five Lions opposed them. They were outnumbered only initially, though, until one of them vanished with the sound of single loud gong strike.

The token nestled in a pile of yellow goo in the center of the chamber. Multiple holes littered the area around the prize, which made it all too easy for a player to fall to their doom. The Lions were closer, but Adrien wouldn't depend on the possibility that a team in the semi-finals might make a clumsy mistake. The Cardinals needed to be proactive and especially so given their reduced numbers.

"We have to make our move," he said. "I'll go for it. Prepare to cover—"

One of the Lions burst toward the token. The elf quickly cast an entanglement spell, but it missed and the player's shield absorbed the strikes from the other Cardinals. The Lion pitched forward as he landed roughly and narrowly missed the token as he fell toward a hole.

Adrien's smug smile vanished as somehow, their opponent managed to twist and snagged the coin before he dropped.

Christie patted her boyfriend's hand as he stared at his baked potato. He didn't have an appetite. He hadn't even wanted to eat with their other friends, but Christie insisted she had to join him for dinner. A boy didn't say no her when she really got going. For one thing, she wouldn't let him get in a word edgewise to actually refuse.

"It's okay, Adrien," she said. "I heard the team. None of them blame you. Not even a little. They all say you're a great captain, maybe even better than Matt."

"I had hoped that maybe they'd allow a new game because of the equipment malfunctions," he murmured. "But because the Lions had a malfunction too, they decided to let the results stand, even though they can't explain it. That's it. We're eliminated." He sighed. "So much for our perfect season." He snorted in disgust.

"I know it hurts, but it's not the end of the world."

"But we were so close to reaching and winning the

championship." The elf slumped in his chair, angry at his own failures as team captain.

Christie shrugged. "Last year, the team was eliminated in the quarter-finals. This year, you were eliminated in the semi-finals. I might not be an expert on sports, but I do know that reaching the semi-finals is better than only the quarter-finals. In other words, you did better this season than you did last season. Not only that, but you have one more season as captain."

Adrien sat up and blinked as he absorbed what she'd said. "You're right. The team tried to tell me that, too, but I didn't want to listen. We might not have made it this year, but I swear we will next year,"

Failure was part of life and part of the competition. He would learn from that failure and use it to make him stronger. Then, he would do the same for his team.

She giggled. "There you go. That's my Adrien."

CHAPTER THIRTY-TWO

"I wish they'd hurry up and arrest her already," Philip grumbled as they settled in at two tables in the dining hall. "I never thought I'd mind being stuck at the school so much, but all the people at the places where I volunteer must think I'm a total flake."

Sara smiled. "Didn't you tell them you're not allowed to leave the school right now?"

"Sure, but what if they don't believe me?" He shook his head. "Stupid chaos witch. She's not even that big a deal, right? It's not like she attacked you. They should allow us to leave the school."

She frowned and Evie sighed.

Raine shrugged. "Eris is dangerous. You can tell she's powerful just from being around her, and I could spend an hour telling you about the stunts she's pulled and the people she's hurt. I'm glad they are careful. I'm sure the PDA will capture her soon. They already expected her, after all."

Adrien looked disgruntled. "I wish I'd been there when

she confronted you." He pantomimed a sword strike. "She might be powerful, but we've faced powerful enemies before."

Cameron glowered. "Me too. I'll show her shifter power."

Evie shivered. "She's so weird and creepy. I don't ever want to see her again."

"I agree," Christie said. "And maybe it's weird to focus on, but I didn't like her sense of style or fashion at all but, you know, if she said she was only trying to do whatever, that would be one thing. But it was like she tried to have a look but then didn't really have a look, and it annoyed me, is all." She shrugged.

They waited for their plates and glasses to appear, having already placed their orders. Being restricted to the school might have its disadvantages, but at least they still had access to quality meals prepared by the best pixie cooks that side of the Mississippi. Or, at least, Raine assumed they were.

She could never decide, even though she'd been at the school for years, whether she felt that magically appearing dishes was whimsical and magical or a waste of magic, but she still liked it. If nothing else, it beat having to wait in a long line.

With a small frown, she looked up. She was so used to the enchanted roof and dome either displaying weather scenes or something impressive and atmospheric that to simply look at nothing but an unadorned area above her felt odd and unnatural. A few lines of light flickered here and there, as if a spell tried to manifest but failed. When the magical dining hall decorations broke down, who was responsible for their repair? She honestly didn't know.

Raine's stomach rumbled. "I can't wait to eat. That's what I get for only having that salad at lunch."

Plates appeared in front of the students. She smiled at hers, expecting lasagna. Her expression turned to a look of confusion. "Huh? What's going on?"

No food lay on her plate. The crockery itself was twisted into a spiral filled with multi-colored fractals beside crude stickman drawings of what appeared to be wizards casting spells. A small orange-yellow figurine of a rabbit sat in the center. When she leaned closer and poked it, she realized the animal wasn't a figurine. It was an al-dente lasagna noodle sculpture.

She blinked. "Hey, do you see th— Woah."

Everyone's plate had transformed into different shapes with varied patterns and colors. All the food had been either refashioned into a new item or a strange hybrid. Each slice of Philip's pizza was baked on one side but completely uncooked on the other. His pepperoni glowed on both sides.

Evie yelped as some of her lettuce crawled away on new thin black legs. She looked at Sara.

The kitsune threw her hands up. "I didn't do anything. This isn't me."

Philip held his pizza up and stared at it in horror. "This isn't cool."

Adrien frowned when his quiche wiggled alarmingly and grew fins. He looked at Sara. "Could this be the work of the Tricksters?"

"I doubt it." Sara pointed a few tables down. Jillian

scowled and attempted to spear a writhing sausage link with her fork.

Murmurs of confusion, surprise, and disgust swelled around the dining hall. Several pixies flew around the room, concerned expressions on their faces. Every dish and meal had been transformed into a horrible wreck, abstract piece of art, or a bizarre exploration of life.

Cameron stared belligerently at the meal he'd actually looked forward to a few minutes before. "What's going on? I can see they might mess up an order or even a table, but this goes well beyond that."

The Gray Elf shouted in triumph as she finally stabbed the sausage. She threw the fork on the table and folded her arms, a look of satisfaction on her face.

Raine winced and looked away as she wondered if Dorvu would show up and protest.

The decorations above finally kicked in, but instead of weather or a decorative scene, the images flipped through random scenes every few seconds. First, there was a barbecue restaurant, then an aquarium, followed by the Arc de Triomphe. A swamp replaced a car wash. Someone's living room gave way to a hospital parking lot. There was no pattern and no clue as to the nature of the underlying malfunction.

She stared in bewilderment for a moment before she looked around for any of the professors. But other than the students, only the pixies were present, and they didn't look like they had any clearer idea what was going on than the increasingly loud protesting teens.

Small specks of light broke away from one of the rotating images above. More joined them after the next few images. The specks coalesced to spell out a rippling message above the diners.

THEY EDUCATE YOU TO BIND YOUR MIND. MAGIC SHOULD BE FREE.

I WILL SHOW YOU BEAUTIFUL CHAOS.

Raine stared at the image and her heart kicked into a gallop. "It's Eris. She's here." She pushed to her feet. "We have to tell the headmistress."

Philip sighed. "But I'm still hungry." He tossed his slice of pizza down. "What a waste."

CHAPTER THIRTY-THREE

Mara examined the now empty dining hall. The haphazardly transformed dishes remained, but the message and rotating slideshow of images had vanished before her arrival. She looked over her shoulder at Xander, who had his wand out and now probed a few of the dishes, a concerned look on his face.

She had asked the pixies to evacuate along with the students. It wasn't right to risk the kitchen staff in a battle against a chaos witch.

The wizard waved his wand over a table and muttered a quick incantation. Bright lines appeared over the dishes and parts of the table. "I've finally found something that worries me more than dark magic. That's the problem with living for a long time. You always find something new to worry about."

"Well?" she asked.

He frowned. "I made an assumption that led to a mistake. I only hope it's not a mistake that leads to anyone getting hurt."

"We'll protect the students," Mara said firmly. "No matter what we have to do."

"Would you care to elaborate on the nature of your mistake?" Agent Oliver also moved from table to table, her mouth tight and her wand out. "We have potentially one of the most dangerous witches in the country toying with this school. Anything you could offer that might help us stop her would be nice, Professor Powell."

Bruce stood near a wall and seemed both concerned and frustrated. Mara could understand. This was a magical problem, and a normal FBI agent couldn't add much help. That was why students such as Raine and William were so important to the future of both the FBI and the country. The PDA had its limits and a particular focus.

The world had moved on. It was time for the government to move on with it.

Xander tapped one of the plates with his wand. "I'm talking about the incident on April 1st. I was so focused on determining whether or not it was related to the Arc Eighty-Eight incident that I overlooked the strange signature of some of the magic."

The headmistress fixed him with an impatient stare. "What do you mean?"

"Although the magic did seem to be related to Jillian's Gray Elf magic, there were...subtle twists in it. I didn't think much of them at the time. I thought the girl had somehow merely twisted her own magic. We've all seen it enough from students here over the years when they screw a spell up."

"But it wasn't only that."

He nodded. "I wanted to establish whether it was her spell, so I focused on the wrong thing."

"You can't find something if you don't even bother to look for it," Bruce interjected.

"Exactly. It was a failure of investigation, not of magic."

Xander cast a quick spell and one of the plates glowed. "I see the same kind of thing in this dining hall. For want of a better description, let's call it a corruption of the main magic beneath. The residual magic on the plates is perfectly consistent with the basic magic set up in the dining hall and the spells used by the pixies, but it also displays the same kind of corruption."

Agent Oliver tightened her free hand into a fist. "Could she be here already? Not only in town but somewhere on the school grounds? If so, we should request that the PDA agents redeploy here."

The FBI agent frowned and stepped away from the wall. "I doubt it. Why wouldn't she make a direct appearance, then?"

"It's a game, maybe?"

He shook his head. "She has run in the past from both the PDA and FBI, but she's also publicly engaged them, especially on her own terms. She's obviously not that concerned about capture since she's gone after students in stores and has corrupted everything."

Mara frowned. "I don't care that she's the Witch Queen of Chaos. Rhazdon herself couldn't get through the new wards without us knowing. Not being able to be tracked isn't the same thing as being immune to magic. We've even set the wards up with the idea that someone might attempt to cloak their magical signature. They aren't fool-proof, but they're damned close."

The other woman scoffed. "You have some powerful magicals here, Headmistress, but you're not gods. This woman has evaded the PDA for years. She has powers and tricks you're not used to. Even though we don't know a lot about the artifact that affected her, it's increased her abilities."

"I'm not saying we're gods, but neither is she a goddess. I'm saying we've taken precautions. If she were on school grounds, we would have detected her in some way or Dorvu would have seen her. Everything you've told me indicates that regardless of what form she's in, she tends to stand out. Raine's encounter only reinforces that. I'm dubious that she's hidden or remained invisible this entire time only to play pranks like she's a member of the Live Unnecessary Tricksters. That's my honest opinion, and especially since she has an ideological objection to this school."

"That's true," Agent Oliver said. "If you can stomach it, you should read some of her manifestos sometime. Organized education, she claims, is the single most destructive element of society."

Eleanor, Leo, Miles, and Annabelle hurried into the dining hall. They all looked out of breath.

Mara sighed. She suspected she already knew what they were about to say. "Did you find anything?"

"There are pockets of unusual magic all over the mansion," the head librarian said with a concerned frown. His poppy growled. "There are minor spell malfunctions all over as well. Nothing dangerous, but the magic's become unstable. I ran into a girl who saw something odd. She thought a spirit had gotten through somehow, but it was only an odd illusion of a dolphin jumping in front of a window. I dispelled it, but it was harder than it should have been."

The headmistress pinched the bridge of her nose. "Eleanor, will you please take the others to the front gate and verify that the glamor is still intact? The last thing we need right now is outside attention. At least Leo's efforts show we can begin to unravel some of what Eris has done now that we know she's done it."

The newly arrived professors turned to leave.

Leo stood fast. "There are a couple of things I want to talk about."

"Feel free to stay." She nodded. "I suspect we'll have a lot to talk about very soon."

The others departed with one last glance at Leo.

Agent Oliver completed her inspection of another plate. "The more I think about it, the more I must admit that Agent Connor is right—and I suspect you're right as well, Headmistress."

"Right about what?" Bruce asked.

She gestured around the room. "Something about this situation feels off. I wonder, now, if this isn't an attempt to mislead us somehow. Even if she's not on campus, she's obviously somehow affected the school. Some of the reported tricks are similar to things she's done, but they lack some of the truly theatrical elements associated with her, which means it's less likely she's actually on campus." She nodded at Xander. "She's spreading this corruption somehow, and it's disrupting things at the school. Even if the staff counter what she's done, we'll need to isolate the cause to truly eliminate it."

"And it has gone on for a while," Mara said. "At least since April 1st and before then." She pursed her lips as she thought back. "The student's magic was affected first, probably because they have less control over it—or, maybe, whatever method she uses targeted them preferentially. That explains some of the problems in class and the bizarre prank disaster. Now, the pixies have issues as well. Victoria told me that most of the food started moving during dinner, shortly before she sent a student to find me. The pixies were able to cancel the magic that animated it, but many of the students were disturbed. I want to open the minds of students, but I don't want to traumatize them."

Leo cleared his throat. "There have been problems with some of the ladders in the library over the last couple of days. I didn't bother you with it because I assumed the spells simply needed to be recharged, but this explains that."

The ghostly laughter of a girl echoed all around them. It was followed by the girl singing, "Ring-around-the-Rosie" slowly.

Bruce snorted. "Now that's simply screwing with us. This isn't funny."

Mara shook her head. "I don't know how much she's chosen what she's done versus merely warped the magic here. As we learned during the Arc Eighty-Eight incident, this school's combination of concentrated magic and proximity to the kemana make it vulnerable to unusual magical occurrences. It may very well be that she's taken advantage of that somehow." She looked at Agent Oliver. "I take it that your associates are no closer to finding her?"

The PDA agent stiffened. "She can't be tracked directly, but additional agents have been sent, and since she's dispensed with stealth, so have we. We're canvassing the area for her directly and looking for unusual magic, but it's difficult to accomplish in a place like that since there is so much unusual magic. Fortunately, the local magical population seems inclined to cooperate."

The headmistress sighed. "With the presumption that she isn't at the school, our safest course of action is to restrict the students to the grounds as she's already proven she's willing to engage them."

Xander squatted and looked underneath a table. "Not that I disagree, but if every student is forced to sit around on their hands and do nothing, that could cause trouble, too—especially with magic disrupted like this."

"I think it's important to have the students continue with their daily lessons. Perhaps we'll dispense with practical spellwork for a few days, but you're right. We can't keep them here and have them do nothing. They shouldn't spend time worrying about Eris. That's not their job."

"No, it isn't." Agent Oliver lifted her chin. "The PDA will capture her. It's a matter of time now. She's so confident that she'll either stay in this area, or she'll keep coming back, which means we'll be able to nail her. You keep the students in line, and we'll do the rest."

"I don't want a battle at this school, Agent Oliver. We've already gone through that once, and I don't want to subject students to that kind of thing."

The other woman scoffed. "Don't worry, Headmistress.

We'll do everything we can to bring that witch into custody. You might care because they're your students, but we're the Paranormal Defense Agency. It's our job to protect the country from magical threats like Eris."

Mara stared at a plate that had been rearranged into a jigsaw puzzle of a gnome wearing a ten-gallon hat. "Right now, I'd settle for you defending this school."

CHAPTER THIRTY-FOUR

Sara sighed as she dashed paint onto her canvas. It had been two days since the cafeteria incident. Although the professors had restored order around campus and the students could have a decent meal without the risk that it would turn into food statues or run away, the tension remained thick.

Everyone waited for Eris' next move. Some students were afraid, but others admired her message and antics. Jillian had admitted that while she didn't like the fact that Eris had hurt people in the past, she wished she could have pulled off a prank similar to what the witch had accomplished in the dining hall. She apparently found some appeal in the idea of chaos challenging order.

The PDA was no closer to making an arrest from what Raine had heard, and the professors didn't want students to even use much magic out of fear that the chaos witch's influence would taint it. Raine had said she was fine with that. From what she understood, it was Eris' fault that she'd almost been killed during the last day of the prank war.

While Sara could understand that, she had worked so long and hard to gain her magic and didn't like the idea that she was unable to use it because of the actions of some witch she'd met for a few minutes in a store.

What was the point of being at a magic school where they didn't let her use magic?

The kitsune tried to convince herself it would be a temporary measure, but the restriction of the students to the school grounds was also supposed to be a temporary measure. It had somehow stretched from days to weeks.

Her friends had decided to get their minds off things with more movie nights. Most of them were already in the movie room setting things up. Sara wanted to add a few touches to her latest work before she joined them. Working on her art always calmed her.

She stared at her palette and sighed. Despite the soothing activity, she knew she was breaking the rules— and arguably channeling a little of the Eris spirit—but it was for a good cause. Her artistic soul needed to be fed.

Besides, while she did use magical paints Caleb had purchased in the kemana, she hadn't experienced any unusual effects or seen anything that made her think it was dangerous. None of her paintings had come to life.

Sara released a long sigh when she thought about Caleb. He had come down with something and passed out in his dorm room the night before. The nurse and professors had stabilized him, but they were afraid to use normal healing magic or potions because of the risk that the spell might backfire and harm him even more. There was some talk of transporting him to a hospital in town.

Normally, illness and injury were a minor concern at the School of Necessary Magic, but everything that made the school special revolved around the very thing they now feared—magic.

The kitsune turned to head around the corner and take another look at a series of acrylic landscapes Caleb had worked on as part of a self-discovery project. He had been adding to the paintings when he fell ill.

He called them the five elements—paintings of a desert vista, an expansive ocean, a tall, snow-capped mountain, a tornado, and a glowing aurora. They were all expertly done on a technical level, but Sara didn't really feel anything when she looked at them. He had never been all that open on what he tried to explore in doing the paintings.

The desert image shifted to a city skyline she didn't recognize.

"Huh?" She frowned.

Caleb had talked about how he would use magic to add a spell component to the paintings, but she hadn't heard him say anything throughout the entire semester about the scenes themselves changing. In addition, she'd seen him working on them without any image alterations. Paintings didn't normally change themselves, even at a magical school.

The ocean shifted to the entrance to a large cave. The mountain changed, and this time, the new image was a place she recognized, if only because she had been there recently.

Sara's eyes widened. It was also hard not to recognize the two blue-haired elves in the picture.

Raine unzipped her coat as she stepped into the art room. She'd come in from outside and had barely reached the movie room when Sara rushed in and demanded everyone's attention, saying she needed to show them something right away in the art room.

The kitsune ran around the corner and gestured for them to follow her. She pointed to a painting.

"Why would Caleb paint a picture of Vianna and Madelyn in the Raven Room? That's kind of weird." Raine leaned forward to look more closely.

"That's just it," Sara said. "He didn't. This picture never looked like that before. This isn't the kind of thing he would normally paint anyway." She gestured to a few other pictures. "They've suddenly all changed. And Caleb's sick, and this Eris stuff is happening. Maybe it's all connected. I wanted to show you all before I went to the headmistress or a professor because I didn't want to cause trouble if I've simply overreacted."

"Randomly changing paintings are the kind of thing you should overreact to." Raine tilted her head as she scrutinized the canvas. Vianna looked angry, but Madelyn looked scared. That wasn't all that surprising.

"A while back, I overheard Vianna talking about finding something. I assumed it had something to do with their parents letting them stay here, but what if I'm wrong? What if they're mixed up with Eris somehow? If she came to them and offered to help them with Madelyn's condition, they might have been too desperate to say no, especially if their parents aren't helping."

Cameron pointed at the artwork. "We don't know anything about what's going on other than that they're in a picture of the Raven Room. That doesn't mean anything." He shrugged. "Think about all the weird stuff that happened in the cafeteria. It didn't have some deep meaning."

The painting shimmered slightly, and Madelyn's image turned. Her hand reached out as if she offered it to Raine.

William frowned, and fire flashed in his eyes. "I don't like this. If those paintings start crawling away, I'll burn them."

Philip backed away, his expression grim and more than a little nervous. "That might not be a bad idea, dude."

Evie retrieved a small sun flare potion from her pocket, a determined look on her face.

Raine held a hand up. "Everyone, calm down. We don't know what's going on. Maybe this is simply one of Eris' little tricks to mess with us." She gestured to the painting. "Just because there's magic doesn't mean this isn't anything more than a picture. But maybe we should find the sisters and ask them." She tapped Madelyn's hand. "If they're lying—"

The painting winked out of existence. Raine squeaked, pitched forward, and knocked the easel over when she bumped it with her knee.

"Ow."

Cameron rushed to her side. "Are you all right?"

Before she could answer, a swirling portal appeared.

Tendrils of light erupted from the gateway and wound around the students. With a quick yank, the thin tentacles hauled them through before they could even understand what had happened.

The seven students fell into the dusty carpet and hardwood floor of the Raven Room in an ungainly pile. The gateway closed behind them, but a massive portal to a grand ballroom was open on the opposite wall.

Raine rubbed her knee and turned to find a scowling Vianna and a cringing Madelyn in the corner.

Vianna narrowed her eyes. "What are you doing here?"

CHAPTER THIRTY-FIVE

The snarky Coral Elf threw her hands up. "Aren't you supposed to stay on campus, Campbell and her Trouble Squad?"

Raine stood and frowned. "I could say the same thing to you. How did you get here without the professors finding out?"

Vianna jabbed a finger in the air. "Let's say that with all Eris' stunts, it was easy to get away if you were ready and waiting for a distraction. But I'm done answering questions. So, why don't you shut up and leave? We don't need your help."

"I'm not going anywhere. You can yell at me and try to make me leave, but it won't work."

The girl sneered. "I don't care who you are. I thought you were okay, but now I know you're nothing more than a suspicious girl who's sniffed around Madelyn again because you're desperate to prove something to your FBI handler. You're ready to sell us out and buy your way into the FBI." She scoffed. "Aren't you, Campbell?"

Cameron stepped up beside his girlfriend and his eyes flashed yellow. He growled a low warning. "Watch it."

"Or what?" Vianna raised a hand. "I'm not defenseless. Bring it, wolf boy."

Madelyn sighed and grabbed her sister's arm. "J-just stop it. I'm tired of lying. We're here looking for an artifact, Raine. It's like Vianna said. We used the distraction of Eris and special magic to make it off campus. That special magic helped, but the wards aren't there to keep people in. They're there to keep people out."

The other elf's eyes bulged. "You're telling them? They'll go straight to Berens and rat us out. You can't trust them."

"Maybe that's a good thing. The headmistress could help us."

Raine offered Madelyn a warm smile. "Everything I told you before was true. All I want to do is help you, but I need you to help me understand what's going on. Why would you need an artifact?"

"Because we'll die without it."

Vianna shook her sister's shoulders. "Stop it. You can't trust them. You can't trust anyone but me, and you know it."

Madelyn batted her hands away and stared at her, rare defiance in her eyes. "I do trust you, but I also want to trust more people than only you." She stepped aside, her eyes now downcast. "Like I said, we need the artifact, or we'll die."

Raine nodded. "Because you're Coral Elves in a low-magic environment?"

"Don't do this, Madelyn." Vianna glared at the other elf.

"I've gotten us this far, haven't I? You know they'll never let us live if they know the truth. You can't count on their mercy."

Madelyn shook her head. "No more lies. No more running. If you want me to stop, then you'll have to kill me." She spread her arms wide. "Go ahead." Her voice wavered. "You promised me w-we could have a life, but we're dying, and I'm not even allowed to have friends. How is it better than there?"

Vianna narrowed her eyes. "Because you at least have me, you stupid idiot." She raised her palm.

The FBI Trouble Squad spread out, several ready to pounce on Vianna. Adrien summoned a sword.

The aggressive elf lowered her arm and slumped against a wall. "Fine then, idiot. Do what you want. Don't cry to me when the PDA executes us."

"You have to understand, Raine, that we met before that first time we met."

Raine frowned, already bewildered. "How do you meet someone before you meet them?"

"By meeting them when they're in a different form." The elf placed her hand over her heart. "You met us when we were still Maeve."

The teens all gasped.

She stared at Madelyn. "That's...not possible. You're Maeve?"

"When the Arc Eighty-Eight pocket dimension started to collapse, we were able to strengthen it. The contents of the world still dissolved, but we were at least able to keep its essence from imploding and destroying us. But what kind of life is that?" She shuddered. "I told you before. It was nothing but endless darkness alone."

Sara looked from the scowling Vianna to her weary sister. "I don't understand how a tutorial fairy becomes two Coral Elves."

"Maeve realized—we realized we couldn't stay in the dark place." Madelyn swallowed. "We didn't want to die, but we couldn't manifest in the real world, not directly, but after a while, we figured it out with some experimentation. We could use most of what was left of our power to become someone real in your world—not a character in a game but someone living and breathing. We knew that magic would leave traces of what we were, and we also knew that you and the professors would be suspicious."

"Why not leave the school, then?" Philip asked with a shrug.

"It's hard. We're not stable. It's like the school itself stabilizes us. It was hard to even go into the kemana." Madelyn sighed. "Coral Elves have different colored eyes, so they were an easy choice, and there aren't a lot around this area, so no one would question our behavior." Her voice grew quiet, and she trembled. "We also realized we couldn't manifest without reducing our power, so we broke apart. One side became the bravery, courage, and fire—the protector. The other, the sensitivity, and the empathy—the heart. One soul became two."

Philip blinked. "Woah. Just...woah."

Evie and Sara watched in silence, shocked expressions on their faces.

Adrien and Cameron stepped back. The elf's sword vanished, and the tension left his face.

Madelyn wiped a few tears away. "We're not fakes, Raine. Not really. We are Coral Elves now. Most of our Maeve magic is gone. We've saved it so we can do things like tonight—let a small part of our old reality overwrite this reality. Magical hacking. But Vianna's right. No one will trust us. We knew no one would accept us because of what we did when we were Maeve, so we had to do all this ourselves and lie about who and what we are. But we didn't want to die or be stuck in that endless darkness." She lowered her head and sobbed.

Vianna sighed and looked away. "You stupid idiot. Now you've done it."

Raine stepped forward and pulled Madelyn into an embrace. She patted her back. "You're not alone now. We can help you."

Cameron grimaced. "She tried to kidnap us and force us to stay in her twisted world."

Vianna snorted. "See, Madelyn? I was right. You can't trust anyone but me."

Raine shook her head. "Maeve's gone. Don't you see? Maeve's not them. She's kind of like a mother who died giving birth to them, and I won't blame the children for the mother's crimes." She continued to pat the elf's back and stroke her hair and turned to Vianna. "The one thing I don't understand is why you brought us here since you obviously don't want us here."

"Brought you here?" the elf scoffed. "We didn't bring you here. We were trying to escape."

William frowned. "Escape from the place you broke into?"

Vianna rolled her eyes. "Try to keep up, Sulfur Butt."

The half-Ifrit grunted. "Then explain better."

"Okay, here's the quick version. We've waited for a particular day. Certain flows of magical energy were building and would reach the level we needed on that day, which is—well, today." She threw her hands up. "I found information about an artifact hidden in a place connected to the Raven Room, something that can help to stabilize us. Once the original magical energy from Maeve is gone, we'll die, but with the artifact, we can continue to live. It's not some big plot or anything. The artifact would be destroyed in stabilizing us. The problem is that stupid chaos witch." She gritted her teeth. "She ruined everything when she showed up out of nowhere. It turns out she wants it, too. I have no idea why. We found what we needed to open that portal on the wall there, but she blocked it from us."

"What about the portal that brought us here?" Raine asked.

Vianna shrugged. "I don't know. It simply appeared. I have no idea why. Do you guys have some special connection to this place?"

Raine gasped and released Madelyn gently, and the elf stepped back and sniffled. She checked her coat pocket. The wooden raven from their last trip was still there and felt hot. "Thanks, Ted."

"Who the heck is Ted?"

"Probably Edgar Allen Poe."

Vianna stared at her. "Are you messing with me?"

Cameron scoffed. "Says the Coral Elf who is actually half the soul of a tutorial fairy from a magical game?"

"Cool it, wolf boy." Vianna pointed to the portal on the

back wall. "That's where we wanted to go. We activated a spell here to open that before Eris ambushed us. We can't get past the forcefield she put up. You might not trust us. I know I don't trust you, but I think we're on the same side here because I'm reasonably sure no one wants that chaos witch to get the artifact."

She shifter narrowed his eyes. "How do we know you won't betray us the minute you have a chance?"

The elf nodded at Madelyn. "Yeah, because she'll rip your heart out like a rabid Kilomea. It's call leverage, wolf boy."

He growled. "We don't take hostages."

"Then stop whining, and let's find a way to get out of here."

Raine approached the portal. She held her hand up and reached toward it. An invisible wall prevented her from coming close. She took a deep breath and moved the wooden raven toward the wall. The portal pulsed, and she was able to move past the invisible barrier.

"I think it's open now."

Evie swallowed. "If we go through there, we'll have to fight Eris."

She nodded. "Probably."

Adrien's sword winked into existence. "So be it."

"She almost killed Raine. We owe her anyway."A fireball appeared in William's palm.

Sara frowned. "She's giving trickster magic a bad name."

"Then let's go, FBI Trouble Squad." Vianna grinned. "I want to see if you've earned the rep."

Raine drew her wand and cast a shield spell over herself. Cameron shifted into wolf form and growled.

"Everyone, be careful," she said softly. "And keep in mind that we have the Princesses of New Arcadia on our side." She turned and smiled at Madelyn and Vianna before she stepped through the portal.

CHAPTER THIRTY-SIX

They emerged into the vast ballroom of what looked like an old colonial mansion that reminded them vaguely of the main School of Necessary Magic building. Raine pointed to a trail of footprints in the thick dust on the door. They led to an open set of double doors and the group rushed in that direction.

The sisters and FBI Trouble Squad entered an even dustier front room. Furniture stood covered with sheets and plastic. Dark stairs spiraled on both sides of the space to a second floor.

A tall, thin woman with blue hair stood behind the railing in denim shorts and a leather jacket. Her wand hung loosely in her right hand. The familiar aura of power was present, even though she didn't look at all like she had the last time they had encountered her.

"Eris," Raine shouted and held her wand at the ready.

Sara fumbled in her back pocket. "It's a good thing I always keep a few acorns and seed in my pockets for emergencies."

"I can't find it," their adversary shouted. "It's not fair. I can't find it." She shook a finger at Raine. "You'd be angry too if you couldn't find it."

"Surrender, Eris," Raine shouted back. "We don't want to hurt you, but you've poisoned the school with whatever you've done, and you're a wanted criminal."

"Forget that. It was all simply for some fun—a way to remind you little children of what magic should be. Those dreadful professors and their awful order are strangling your magic." Eris clucked her tongue and waved her wand. "But I offer freedom. Not the chains they would put on you."

Vianna shook her fist. "Listen, you crazy witch. My sister and I need that artifact, and if I have to go through you to get it, that honestly won't be a problem. Do you understand?"

The chaos witch laughed. "Wonderful. Fight for your life." Her face contorted into a frown. "False order. I see it. I sense it." She pointed her wand at each Coral Elf in turn. "Fakes. You should have stayed in the chaos."

Madelyn winced. "We're not fakes."

"Bite me," Vianna shouted. "We might be fakes, but at least we're not some whacked-out witch who thinks messing with a school is fun. All this garbage about order and chaos aside, you're merely some woman who got lucky and wants to do whatever she feels like."

Eris flicked her wand and pointed it backward. The wall rippled behind her like water. "Let's have some fun. I'll give you some friends to play with. Then, you can catch me if you can."

Cameron crouched and growled.

The chaos witch stepped through the wall.

Vianna rolled her eyes. "She's really annoying."

Everyone looked up at the sound of soft thuds. Pink rubber balls bounced down both sets of stairs. The teens backed away as a group. The balls reached the lower level and crude arms and legs sprouted from them.

Philip chuckled. "Those are kind of cute."

With a flash, the ball men turned from tiny to over seven feet tall. Gangly, long limbs with only three fingers were attached to an elongated and featureless torso. A giant rubber ball served as the head.

Raine blinked. "I didn't expect that."

"Like I said," Vianna muttered. "Really annoying."

The newcomers charged without preamble. Cameron met the first enemy and ripped into his leg, only to find more rubber.

Raine fired a magical bolt at one of them. The missile charred the upper-layer of material, but the creature didn't display any pain or react in any way.

Sara threw a seed at both groups. Vines sprouted and snagged several of the ball men to trap them.

Evie stuck her sun flare potion in her pocket and retrieved her wand. Vianna thrust out her palm and coated the floor in front of the stairs with ice. Several of the enemy slipped and fell.

Madelyn crouched with her hands over her face and trembled.

Adrien severed the arm from an enemy, but the ball man didn't even react as it swung a fist toward him. He ducked and sliced off the other arm. The attacker kicked at him, and the elf proceeded to hack it into pieces with deft strokes.

Philip laughed as he dismembered his opponent with a few rapid cut spells. "This is totally like the Black Knight from *Monty Python and the Holy Grail*."

Evie and Raine soon adopted his tactics.

"I hate that movie," Adrien sneered as he eliminated another adversary.

"I know. You told us that at least ten times when we watched it."

Cameron savaged another pile of rubber. Although the pieces of the crude men twitched after separation, they ceased all movement after a minute or so.

William kicked at a scorched mass of rubber at his feet. "That wasn't so bad. The PDA can't handle that?"

Raine pointed to a wall upstairs that rippled and wavered. "We need to catch up." She stepped gingerly over the patch of ice before she raced up the stairs. Everyone else followed on either side, and Madelyn trailed the group, still shaking in terror.

They stepped through the undulating barrier and into a long white hallway that ran in either direction with no sign of the wall they'd entered through. The only defining feature was the worn, ancient hardwood floors.

They barreled ahead and expected a turn, but after a minute, they slowed when there was no sign of either a turn or a door.

"Something's wrong," Raine said. "We should have found a room or something by now. Did we go the wrong way?"

Adrien carved an X in the floor. "I have an idea. Let's keep going this way."

The group continued but in less than thirty seconds, they reached Adrien's mark even though they had moved forward the entire time.

"It wraps around on itself?" Sara groaned. "That's not fair."

Cameron growled and clawed at a wall.

Raine looked back and forth. "If it simply circles in on itself, then what—we're trapped here?"

Vianna kicked the wall. "That was probably the witch's plan. For a woman who acts so kooky, she sure plans well."

Cameron shifted into human form. "But she got out."

Raine nodded. "And according to the PDA, she can portal."

Evie looked at William with concern. "What do we do, then?"

The shifter pointed at Vianna. "What about Maeve magic? Can't you portal?"

"We don't have enough left, wolf boy." The Coral Elf shrugged. "We didn't even open the portal in the Raven Room. If we try that now, we die."

Philip kicked the bottom of the wall and dented it. He grinned. "Maybe if we can't go straight ahead, we should change direction." He raised his wand. "Everybody, step away from the wall."

William raised his arms while Raine and Evie aimed their wands. Adrien and Sara moved back to leave the temporary renovation work to their friends.

The wizard smiled. "I've always wanted to say this—fire in the hole!"

The combined fireballs from the wizard, witches, and half-Ifrit exploded a massive, smoking hole in the barrier. Madelyn yelped and stumbled back.

Cameron waved smoke out of his face and stepped through the aperture. They'd opened a path to another long, mostly featureless hallway, this one with tiled floors.

"I don't know if we're getting somewhere or if this is a big joke."

Raine pushed through behind him. "It can't go on forever. Let's go. We need to catch up with Eris."

CHAPTER THIRTY-SEVEN

She was right. It couldn't go on forever. After they'd blasted through five walls, they somehow ended up back in the ballroom. It didn't make sense from a geometry standpoint, but many things had made no sense in the last several minutes.

"Someone, call Noel Tucker," Philip said. "We need a better magical architect for this place."

Raine looked around, her expression grim. "Where is Eris?"

Evie pointed at a back door to the ballroom that was now open. It led outside.

The chaos witch stood in the middle of a huge, weed-strewn feed yard with lavender-blue flowers. She muttered to herself. Even from a distance, the huge amounts of magical energy that pulsed from the area were clearly visible.

The teens hurried from the mansion and fanned out. Cameron shifted into wolf form once more. Madelyn took her usual position behind everyone, her face even paler than normal.

Eris waved at them. "Hello again. I've almost found it. I'm so looking forward to this."

Vianna frowned. "You found the bell in a garden? That doesn't make any sense."

"Yes." The witch took a few steps, knelt, and inhaled deeply, smiling. "I was misled. It wasn't a bell. No, not a bell at all."

The Coral Elf's face tightened.

Raine looked at her. "You were looking for a bell?"

"Yeah, there was supposed to be a bell here that my information said would give 'life to that which had none.' I figured it would work to help us."

Evie's eyes widened. "Do you know what kind of flowers those are?" She pointed to the lavender-blue flowers.

"No, why? What does that even matter? I'm not here flower shopping, O'Connor."

"Those are Virginia Bluebells."

Vianna rolled her eyes. "Seriously?"

Eris spun with her arms stretched out. "Look at me, I'm Julie Andrews." She stopped and her eyes widened, a faint smile on her face. "I can almost smell the flower now. Oh, how it glows." She raised her wand and whispered a spell. A pulsating aura surrounded her.

Raine couldn't make out the glowing flower from her position and kept her wand pointed at Eris. "Give it up. You'll surrender, and we'll contact the PDA. I don't know why you need some magic life-giving flower, but I'm sure it's not for anything good."

The chaos witch turned toward her and regarded her with a challenging tilt to her head. "Stop me, then. Show me the power of order, Little Miss FBI."

She looked at her friends, and they nodded. Confident, she raised her wand and cast a restraint and entangling spell. She expected rope to appear, but instead, she produced a stream of large bubbles.

Eris patted her chest. "Go ahead. Stop me. Come on, now. That's seriously sad."

William brought his hand back and threw it forward as if to launch a fireball. Dirt rather than flame left his palm, and it didn't reach his target.

"How does she do that?" The half-Ifrit gritted his teeth.

Adrien and Cameron thrust into the attack simultaneously. Their adversary flung her arm with the wand up. The ground beneath them exploded in a cloud of dirt, confetti, and raisins.

The odd transfiguration would have been more amusing if the force of the retaliation hadn't hurled the two friends back so hard that they crashed into the outside wall of the mansion and left actual indentations.

The elf groaned and pushed to his knees. Blood trickled down his face. While his shield had protected him from the full force of the attack, he wasn't seriously injured.

Cameron growled and shook his head to clear it.

Eris sighed and stuck her bottom lip out. "Why are you trying to stop me? Because they have told you how awful I am? Because they say I'm a bad person? Don't you understand that once I have the power of the flower, my creations will receive true permanence? I'll be able to truly carry out my mission to make the world a better place."

"To bring freedom to magic?" Raine asked. She shook her head. "I've read your manifestos. They're nonsense. They're so bad, they're not even worth debating. I don't know how you think being able to make rubber ball men who last longer will help with that. To be honest, I don't care. You've hurt people, and we're here to stop you right here and right now."

The witch waved her wand disdainfully. "That's the problem with that school and all those who have established these limits. Magic is raw creation. Only when you truly embrace the truth that that magic changes reality can you live up to its potential. As I did."

Philip crept in front of Evie as she fished out her sun flare potion. "That's garbage. You didn't get stronger because you accepted anything. You merely found some artifact and it turbocharged you. The irony is that it was probably made by some wizard who went to a place like the School of Necessary Magic."

"Because I kept up an open mind. Duh." Eris rolled her eyes. "Don't you see? You should see. You're still children. The world hasn't changed like it should have. It's still very much the same. The same countries. The same rules. Magic should set this planet free, but they have only found new ways to create new shackles. I offer beautiful chaos that will set you free. That will set everyone free."

Raine snorted. "Your beautiful chaos has killed people. It almost killed me."

The fugitive witch took a few steps backward. "And I'm truly sorry. The path of chaos is not for those who always seek happy endings. The only thing I can offer is the truth of existence."

Vianna's arm jerked up, and she pointed behind the woman. "It's there. I can see it. Just let me get it, and I can end this."

William frowned. "Or kill us all to cover your tracks."

Sara sighed. "We still have the problem of the Witch Queen of Chaos there."

Eris watched them with a playful smile on her face.

Raine took a few steps back and lowered her voice. "Nothing direct works, so we shouldn't try anything direct."

"Meaning what?" the kitsune asked.

"Distraction and that kind of thing." She grinned. "Kitsune magic is kind of chaotic. Go indirect with that. The rest of us target around her, not her directly. At least if Vianna has the flower, she might not want to risk more attacks."

Madelyn swallowed. "This is too dangerous. Vianna, tell them to go. I don't want them hurt."

"You're ready to die because you're worried about these fools?" her sister snorted.

"Geez, thanks." Sara rolled her eyes.

Raine smiled at the timid elf. "This isn't only about you anymore. We can't let Eris get that flower. If she's already this powerful and unstable, it'll be ten times worse if she can create an army by combining her powers with the flower. No, we'll go with the plan. I'll start. When I raise my wand, look away." She turned toward their target.

The witch shrugged. "I assume you've made some clever plans. Played your soldier games. Let's see it."

Raine whipped her wand up, shouted a spell, and closed her eyes. Her wand flashed brightly.

Vianna flung herself into the tall grass and crawled forward.

Sara acted next. She aimed slightly to Eris' side and hurled an acorn. When it struck the ground, it exploded in a shower of crackling sparks.

William tossed several firebolts around the flowers. Flames leapt from plant to plant and dark smoke billowed up.

Adrien rushed forward and Cameron sprinted alongside him. The elf cast a burst spell a few yards away from the witch and flew over her.

Eris twirled her wand. "Not very nice."

A giant glowing tennis racket appeared and batted him away. He hissed in pain as he catapulted back and crashed through a second-story window. The racket swung again and hurled the shifter through the same window.

Eris snapped her wrist, and the racket disappeared. "Oops. I think that's out of bounds." She cut through the air with her wand. The back wall behind the teens exploded in a shower of sunflower seeds, both natural and those made of different materials, including metal.

The shields of the FBI Trouble Squad protected them from serious injury, but the attack brought them to their knees.

Madelyn whimpered in pain. Blood trickled down her side from multiple metal shards embedded in the flesh.

Vianna sat upright, her eyes wide. "Madelyn!"

Eris' amused gaze ticked over to the Coral Elf. "Trying to surprise me. That's better. More creative. You're good for a fake."

Adrien swung out of the second-floor window and

rappelled down with a light rope. Cameron bounced onto the roof below and from there, into the garden. Both were wounded but not disabled.

Madelyn rolled onto her side and sobbed in pain.

Raine turned toward Eris. Her hands twitched and her heart pounded. "This ends, witch. Everyone, keep with the plan. We can do this."

Their adversary grinned and sashayed a few steps back. "You do realize you haven't even hurt me? So brave but so pointless."

"We don't need to hurt you to win. And I understand that now. Whatever you've done at the school, it's limited to the school. Our magic works fine here unless we go after you directly. We'll stop you, even playing on your own terms."

"Because you're students of the School of Necessary Magic?"

Sara stepped forward and readied a handful of seed. "No, because we're the FBI Trouble Squad."

CHAPTER THIRTY-EIGHT

Evie hurled her sun flare potion. It cracked against Eris' shield but produced no light, only a sea of foam instead. "Okay, that works."

Raine aimed her wand above the chaos witch and summoned slime. The sticky deluge coated their adversary's shield.

Vianna sprinted forward and remained parallel to Eris.

The witch screamed in delight. "Now we're having fun. Good job!"

Sara hurled her seeds at random. Vines snaked toward Eris but withered when they touched her protective barrier.

Adrien's sword vanished, and he quick-cast several restraint spells of ropes and chains and launched them in Eris' general direction without aiming. Philip did the same.

The flames spread and the smoke billowed to block the target when the wind blew. The witch threw her head back and laughed and slime still coated her shield.

Cameron resumed his human form and snatched up a

rock. He hurled it toward her, but it bounced off her barrier.

The FBI Trouble Squad maintained the barrage of attacks, not to wound but rather all designed to distract.

Vianna took her opportunity and ducked to avoid notice. She hastily plucked a glowing Bluebell a few yards behind the chaos witch before she turned toward the mansion. A powerful air burst launched her to land hard near Madelyn.

"We've won, Eris," Raine shouted. "We have the flower. If you attack us, you could damage it."

The witch's smile faded. The slime burned off her shield. She looked behind her and then at the Coral Elves. "So you do, but I thought you planned to arrest me, Little Miss FBI. You can't do that simply because you have a flower."

"Stopping you from getting what you wanted is good enough." Raine licked her lips nervously. "Cameron, pick Madelyn up. We need to get her out of here."

None of them knew healing magic that would be good enough to tend to such a serious injury.

Vianna frowned. "She won't last that long. I'm done with these games. I'm done with all of you." She held the flower up and knelt beside her wounded sister.

Cameron narrowed his eyes. "I knew she would betray us."

Eris cocked an eyebrow. "And what do you intend to do, fake?"

The elf made no reply and shoved the entire bloom in the mouth of the half-conscious Madelyn. She placed her hand on her sister's heart and closed her eyes.

The chaos witch tilted her head and scowled with displeasure. "What are you doing?"

A nimbus of blue energy surrounded Vianna and expanded into Madelyn. The flower sizzled into a liquid and dripped down the wounded elf's throat. Her wounds healed instantly, and her entire body glowed.

Vianna gritted her teeth. She grew less substantial and almost translucent.

Raine blinked. "I don't understand what's happening."

Madelyn groaned, and her eyes fluttered open. She gasped. "Vianna, what have you done?"

The elf smiled at her sister. "All I've done is keep to the plan I always had. I lied to you from the beginning, you know."

"See!" Cameron scoffed.

Vianna looked over her shoulder. "Be quiet, wolf boy." She looked at Madelyn. "There was never a way to stabilize us both. I knew that from the minute we separated. I knew I could stabilize you using my magical energy, but I needed a catalyst. The flower wouldn't be enough. It always had to be this way."

Madelyn's eyes widened. "Then, wait…this entire time, you planned—"

"Yes. I've been a bad sister. I know that." Vianna sniffled. A few tears trickled down her fading face. "But I figured I could make it up if I could give you a future."

The other elf teared up. "Don't leave me alone. I can't bear it."

Vianna nodded toward Raine. "You wanted to be Campbell's friend so badly. Then do it. Somehow, I'm convinced that busybody will make sure that you're all right. Won't you, Campbell? Swear it to me."

Raine lowered her wand. "I will. I swear it."

"I'm sorry, Madelyn, for all the pain I put you through." Vianna shimmered and flickered in and out of being, then simply vanished.

No one spoke. The elf had been there one moment and was gone in the next as if she had never even existed.

Madelyn wound her arms around her legs and sobbed.

The FBI Trouble Squad lowered their weapons and most of them wept as well. Tears even pricked the corners of Adrien's eyes.

"No!" Eris screamed. "*No!*"

Raine wiped tears away and pointed her wand at her. "It's over. Don't you get it? It's gone now. Your whole plan was to get the flower. It's done. You've lost and some-body…died today. Isn't that enough?"

The chaos witch laughed, a shrieking, almost inhuman sound. "A fake died. A doll. And she dares to take what I need for my crusade?" She pointed at the sobbing Madelyn. "The power's still in that one, though. If I can't have the Bluebell, I'll drain it from her."

Raine glared defiance. "Over my dead body."

Eris' smile vanished, and she raised her wand. "If I can't free you, then you leave me no choice."

CHAPTER THIRTY-NINE

The fugitive witch waved her wand, and the burning flames in the yard vanished.

Raine tried to cast another slime spell, but before she finished, tendrils of grass as strong as rope twined upward and ripped her wand from her hand. They wound around her wrists and yanked her arms back.

Cameron shifted and attacked while Adrien supported him from afar with a few magical bolts. The attacks changed direction at the last moment.

Several flowers whirled together to form a thin, blue, roughly humanoid creature. The plant monster back-handed the shifter as he launched himself at Eris. He somersaulted to land hard on his head and was knocked unconscious.

Sara threw more seeds, but Eris simply pointed her wand and smiled. The kernels created a barred cage that dropped around the kitsune.

Philip rushed to his girlfriend, only for a seed arm to

take hold of him and yank him into the prison. The limb spun his wand out of his hand.

"Oh, come on," he shouted and shook the bars.

Raine ripped her arm free from the grass bonds and snatched her wand from the ground. They were losing badly, but she refused to let anyone else die.

The chaos witch took a step forward and her smile returned. She waved her wand in dramatic gestures and didn't even bother with any incantations.

New monsters appeared, small familiars of wood, dirt, rock, and plant matter. They overran Adrien, pinned him down, and bounced on his trapped form with glee.

Several of the familiars surrounded the elf and danced in a circle. Raine shook her head, confused by the sight.

"Don't you understand what I am?" Eris shouted. "I am chaos. I am a force of nature. You cannot defeat a force of nature with rules and plans."

William concentrated and a white-hot ball of flame appeared between his hands. Their enemy sighed and flourished her wand.

The boy sagged and fell forward, and immediately, his hands sank into the soil. He stopped moving with only a few inches to spare before his mouth was covered.

"Pointless," the witch muttered. "You should embrace freedom, not ignorance." She continued toward the crying Madelyn. "If that means that I must be harsh, then consider it a lesson in how much love and respect I have for the world."

Raine was the only person still active. She had her wand in her hand but given the utter failure of all her previous attacks, she wasn't sure what she could do. Something burned her side and she hissed in response. She patted her pocket. The raven was burning hot.

The small wooden bird burned through her pocket and fell. She had barely sensed any magic from it before, but now, a tremendous amount poured off it.

"Come on, Ted. I don't even know how the lighthouse story ended. Help me out here."

Multiple portals opened, and Eris turned toward them, genuine surprise on her face.

Raine saw her opportunity and raised her wand. She delivered another quick slime spell and again aimed over and not directly at her adversary. The thick slime coated her shield.

The witch lashed out with her wand. An explosion ripped through a wall in the mansion, but the damage was nowhere near Raine's friends or the portals. The Witch Queen of Chaos was, at least for now, blinded.

"Thank you, Professor Powell," Raine murmured.

PDA agents rushed out of one gateway, led by Agent Oliver, with their wands in hand. Headmistress Berens emerged from another, followed by Professor Powell, Agent Connor, Professor Hudson, Professor Regency, Librarian Decker, and Joe. A huge wolf emerged last— Professor Hodges. Everyone but Mara and Professor Hodges began to chant.

Glowing circles formed around Eris.

"No!" She swung her wand again. Another section of the house exploded and showered the area with wood fragments. The slime finally sizzled off her shield.

The magical reinforcements continued their chant, and

additional circles appeared. Eris tried to cast another spell, but it fizzled in almost the moment that it flared.

Mara raced to the seed cage. She placed her hand on the enclosure and shouted an incantation. The barriers vanished.

"Thanks, Headmistress," Philip said.

Sara sighed with dramatic relief.

The other students were hastily freed with the help of a few counter-spells.

Cameron stirred and shifted into his human form but sat and groaned and held his head. His eyes narrowed on the screeching Eris and a satisfied smile settled on his lips.

Agent Oliver broke away from the chanting agents and retrieved a set of handcuffs impregnated with crystal. Raine had read about them—anti-magic handcuffs. They weren't perfect and couldn't suppress all power, but combined with binding rituals, they could effectively keep a magical under control until the prisoner could be delivered to the appropriate facility for processing.

The PDA agent wore the biggest smile Raine had seen from her as she knocked the chaos witches' wand out of her hand and dragged her arms behind her back.

She slipped the cuffs on. "Lisa Jameison aka Eris. You're under arrest." She rattled off a series of impressive charges, many of which Raine hadn't even heard of despite studying with Agent Connor.

Eris stared at Raine. "You distracted me. You let them bind me. You insolent, foolish, stupid little girl. Do you realize what you've done? You've upset the balance. You've let order win."

She stood, a defiant look on her face. "That was the point, actually."

The prisoner laughed. "This doesn't end. You haven't won. Chaos is eternal."

"So is justice." She tilted her chin in obstinate challenge.

Agent Connor studied her and the concern in his eyes turned to pride.

Mara frowned and looked around. "I see Madelyn, but where is Vianna?"

Raine looked away and the tears threatened to return. Not all victories came without sacrifice.

Madelyn looked up her, her cheeks stained with tears. "Vianna's dead."

CHAPTER FORTY

A few days later, Agent Oliver sat in front of Mara's desk. "You've cleared it all out? Are you sure? We can bring agents in to do a sweep if you think it will help."

The headmistress nodded. "Thank you, but that's unnecessary. My staff has performed that job admirably. You see, Eris used a combination of different objects as resonance sources for the chaos spells. Paints in the art room, some snacks purchased from the kemana...all sorts of different items. The planning and patience of the woman are frightening, especially given how much she claims she's only an agent of chaos. She must have hidden in the kemana for weeks while she planted some of these objects with the students." She sighed. "Fortunately, the few that became ill because of her spell, including Caleb, have recovered."

"All terrorists have their excuses and their fancy philosophical justifications. It always comes down to hurting people and killing them in the end." The agent smiled triumphantly. "We have her secure for now, so it doesn't matter what her plans were. By the time her trial is over, she'll spend so many years in an ultramax that the gates will be fully open when she gets out. This is one time where order beats chaos."

"That's good to hear." Mara sighed. "If only this hadn't ended with a death."

"A death? Oh, you mean Vianna?" Agent Oliver sighed. "We have rather an issue with regard to the other artificial girl."

The headmistress frowned. She didn't like the term and it had dangerous implications.

"So you told me before." She shrugged. "Given the vast diversity of life on Oriceran and how we've been able to handle it here on Earth, I don't see that it matters how she was born. It's not as if PDA research is so advanced that they would learn much from studying her."

"It matters because there's unclear legal ground around the girl." The woman frowned. "No one knows if she should even legally be considered a person. We have many laws about summoned beings, but they don't seem to apply in this case. She's not technically a summoned being. She's a spontaneously generated being." She shrugged. "I'll leave that to Congress to decide."

"She's suffered enough, hasn't she?" Mara frowned. "I don't think taking that poor girl off to some holding facility serves justice or the country. Whatever she was before, she's now merely a grieving Coral Elf."

"Oh?" Agent Oliver smile slightly. "Then what would you suggest, Headmistress?"

"She can stay here at the School of Necessary Magic. I

can't think of a better way to educate a young magical, regardless of her background."

The agent's smile turned victorious. "And you would be willing to take responsibility for her? Even if she isn't Maeve anymore, you know what they say about the fruit of the poisonous tree. We also still have no idea what the implications of her sister's ritual are. She might end up more powerful than Eris for all we know."

The headmistress narrowed her eyes. "Yes, I will take responsibility for her."

Agent Oliver shrugged. "Fine."

"Fine?" Her brow lifted. She wasn't used to the PDA agent giving up so easily.

"That was my recommendation to my superiors, actually. It causes us the least amount of hassle, anyway, given the legal uncertainties. Despite the way I was messing with you, she's obviously not a threat to anyone the way she is now. Based on everything we know, she's technically a baby. You might not like me, Headmistress, but I'm not the kind of woman who would throw a baby in prison."

"I'm surprised." Mara smiled. "Thank you, but I'm even more surprised because I was half-convinced that you didn't trust us here and would submit a report to the government to recommend our shutdown. Yet now, you trust us with new and rare magical life."

"The gnome witness who came forward to tell us about the portal link Raine carried was helpful, but we could still have taken heavy casualties when we first arrived. You saw the kind of things she was capable of. Raine Campbell's quick thinking distracted Eris long enough for us to initiate the binding ritual." Agent Oliver's face tightened. "It's the difference between only Vianna dying and potentially a half-dozen more people dying or being seriously injured." She looked down and shook her head. "This entire year, as I investigated your school, I looked at the wrong things. I looked at the staff and for signs of corruption, but I should have focused on the product."

"The product?"

She nodded. "The students. If you can continue to produce students like the FBI Trouble Squad, then this country will be in good hands in the future. This is a good school, and you're good teachers."

"I'm very happy to hear you say that."

CHAPTER FORTY-ONE

Raine sat across from Madelyn at a table in the library. "I heard they're letting you stay."

The elf nodded slightly, pain in her eyes. "They say that for now, as long as I stay in the school or Ruby Falls, they don't care. Headmistress Berens will work with me to arrange things with the government—like if I actually count as a real person or not."

"Of course you're a real person. You're alive and have real feelings."

"I hated Vianna a lot, you know. At times." She sniffled. "I thought she was simply being mean to me, but that entire time, she planned all this and tried to be strong for me."

Raine gave her hand a comforting squeeze. "I'm truly sorry for your loss but remember my promise to your sister. I'll be your friend, and my friends will be your friends. You'll never have to be alone again. You'll never have to go to a dark place. That's what it means to have friends."

Madelyn teared up. "I'm scared, Raine. I don't know what'll happen now. Vianna had the answers, and I'm merely the coward who followed her."

She shook her head firmly. "No one has all the answers. All you can do is do your best, depend on your friends, and keep moving forward. We'll be here for you." She squeezed her hand again. "And it's all right to feel sad."

The elf burst into tears.

Raine walked around the table, hugged the girl, and stroked her hair. "It's all right. Let it out."

She understood what it meant to lose family because she was an orphan. Madelyn was an orphan, too, in a sense.

Friends and family. Community bonds. That's what made a person truly strong. That's what Eris never understood.

Raine teared up. She missed her mom and dad.

Weeks later, Raine waited alongside Sara and Evie for the jitney. "This might have been our craziest semester yet."

Sara laughed. "You can say that again. I almost don't want to leave."

Raine smiled. "It's only a month until we see each other again for the summer research project."

"Maybe if we're on an island in Maine, we won't run into crazy chaos witches." Evie grinned.

They looked at one another for a moment and burst out laughing.

"Nope!" Raine declared. "I'm sure something crazy will happen in Maine, too, but at least we'll be together."

．　．　．

The story is far from over. Raine's senior year begins and the adventures continue in <u>Untouchable Witch.</u>

For Hire: Teachers for special school in Virginia countryside.

Must be able to handle teenagers with special abilities.

Cannot be afraid to discipline werewolves, wizards, elves and other assorted hormonal teens.

Apply at the School of Necessary Magic.

I was at a birthday party for my neighbor, also named Martha, last night with a lot of different neighbors, different ages, different everything. In the short six months I've lived here we've become a kind of family. This new place I've moved to, into my dream house, has a weird alchemy going. People keep looking for different ways to meet each other. Last week my neighbor down the street put out a Facebook posting to set up a regular Wednesday meet and greet up by the trolley. Highest hill for miles around and on a Wednesday evening, the perfect place to be. I even got to hold two-year-old JoJo who rested her head on my shoulder and didn't want to go back to Dad. A wonderful new nest.

I have lived in six states (seven if I can include all the summers at the Jersey shore) and a lot more towns and cities. I've figured out that I don't do well in high rises. I like to get to know my neighbors, talk to people and here's a general fact – people in high rises move there because they don't like to talk to random strangers – like their neighbors. I never felt so lonely as I did sitting on the 8th floor in NYC.

I've found my favorite places by standing still for just a moment in the location and feeling the energy. I'll pause here for those who need to roll their eyes. Okay, back to this tale. When I moved to Chicago I had very little money, only a bureau, a bed and two and a half chairs and was smack in the middle of the Great Recession. I had spent a month between apartments at a cousin's house in Virginia with a promise that I'd move in 30 days. The stress levels were a little high.

But I stood in that older, elevated first floor apartment in Lincoln Square, closed my eyes and realized I could even take a deep breath. I was finishing ghost writing someone's life story, consulting on other work (read as piecing together just enough work to pay the bills), about to turn fifty. I had so many reasons to just worry in general, and instead I could tell I'd found my next nest. By the time I moved five years later I was friends with all my neighbors (still in touch with some of them, did a reference for another for a job), had seen them all at one point in their pajamas at the mailboxes and felt like I had a family.

For some reason on the next move I ignored that I had always lived in cities and was more relaxed among the hustle and bustle than out where there's space. I moved to a small town outside of Austin and that same kind of high-rise loneliness set in. Very nice town, lots of great activities but not my place. It took me four years to realize I needed to be about thirty miles to the south.

Okay, back to that birthday party. This may turn out to be my last move. I know it's not wise for me to make that kind of declaration. But it's possible I have found a place where I can put down some real and lasting roots, forever – or at least as long as forever turns out to be. Watch JoJo grow up, learn about herbs some more from Heather, finally get the basics of poker and Buddhism from Steve, maybe a homemade wand from Nicole, and drink lemoncella with Elaine. You get the idea – family.

More adventures to follow.

THANK YOU for not only reading this story but these Author Notes as well.

(I think I've been good with always opening with "thank you." If not, I need to edit the other Author Notes!)

RANDOM (sometimes) THOUGHTS?

So, I just had dinner on the coast of the Mexican Baja in Cabo San Lucas with author Russell Blake.

(He writes the JET series)

The food at The Office (a flank steak with vegetables) was fantabulous. The water would occasionally flow up the sand to about five feet of our table, and I watched it pretty hard. I didn't want to become a wet author whatsoever.

I'm older and getting wet wasn't on my list of activities for the night. As an older guy, I have to admit that I'm now refining my taste in activities to ones I know Iike and staying away from ones (like wet jeans with sand inside them) I don't like.

Out in the water was (I'm told) the personal yacht for a

famous golfer (the ship was at least three stories with a helicopter on the back.) Other ships for the tourists were floating around as the sun sank lower and the mountains blocked the light, dropping us into the shadows pretty quickly.

I'm blessed to be able to visit Cabo for a week, and still work. I'm doing (at best) half-days here, and I am very pleased.

I do 3/4 days usually. As in, I'm working for 3/4's of the day and asleep for the other 1/4.

Here, I'm working but instead of the operations work, I'm reading a lot more. It helps to rejuvenate the mind and allows me to decompress as the day moves on. It's just harder for me to stay in the same intense work mode here in Cabo as I would in Vegas or Los Angeles.

I'm hoping that I get the next books story worked out by Saturday morning (It's actually due on Friday, but I don't see me pushing that hard... It's "mañana" time.)

As Craig Martelle would say, Peace fellow humans - Until next time, I'm outta here.

AROUND THE WORLD IN 80 DAYS

One of the interesting (at least to me) aspects of my life is the ability to work from anywhere and at any time. In the future, I hope to re-read my own Author Notes and remember my life as a diary entry.

Inside a metal tube flying over the Sea of Cortez heading to Cabo San Lucas.

So, flying over the Sea of Cortez (I'm told Jacques Cousteau once called it the most beautiful place he ever visited) and I'm reminded that our planet is beautiful. Not only the blue parts, but I'm starting to enjoy the brown parts as well.

Baja California Sur (flying down from Los Angeles) seems to be a very long stretch of mountainous land with a whole heaping lot of brown. My mind starts to wonder whether or not we (humans) will have the engineering capability to make the mountainous land usable for massive engineering projects? If so, add desalinization and we have plenty of land space to add structures.

However, that is the creative in me trying to imagine a future where we easily solve mankind's problems. Then the pragmatic part of my personality kicks in, and I come up with all sorts of challenges which make the idea hard to implement.

That's when the creative side has a serious pout in annoyance about 'challenge this' and 'problem that' and desires to have infinite money to fix these problems.

Anyway, that was a little insight into my mind as I fly. Not exactly the most exciting I admit, but then in the future I wonder if I'll ever read these notes and think "Oh yeah, they just had the first hotel use 3D printing to do exactly this…"

FAN PRICING

$0.99 Saturdays (new LMBPN stuff) and $0.99 Wednesday (both LMBPN books and friends of LMBPN books.) Get great stuff from us and others at tantalizing prices.

Go ahead, I bet you can't read just one.

Sign up here: http://lmbpn.com/email/.

HOW TO MARKET FOR BOOKS YOU LOVE

Review them so others have your thoughts, tell friends and the dogs of your enemies (because who wants to talk with enemies?)… Enough said ;-)

Ad Aeternitatem,

Michael Anderle

OTHER SERIES IN THE ORICERAN
UNIVERSE:

SCHOOL OF NECESSARY MAGIC
THE DANIEL CODEX SERIES
I FEAR NO EVIL
THE UNBELIEVABLE MR. BROWNSTONE
THE LEIRA CHRONICLES
REWRITING JUSTICE
THE KACY CHRONICLES
MIDWEST MAGIC CHRONICLES
SOUL STONE MAGE
THE FAIRHAVEN CHRONICLES

OTHER BOOKS BY JUDITH BERENS

OTHER BOOKS BY MARTHA CARR

**JOIN THE ORICERAN UNIVERSE FAN GROUP ON
FACEBOOK!**

BOOKS BY MICHAEL ANDERLE

For a complete list of books by Michael Anderle, please visit

www.lmbpn.com/ma-books/

All LMBPN Audiobooks are Available at Audible.com and iTunes. For a complete list of audiobooks visit:

www.lmbpn.com/audible

CONNECT WITH THE AUTHORS

Martha Carr Social

Website: http://www.marthacarr.com

Facebook: https://www.facebook.com/ groups/MarthaCarrFans/

Michael Anderle Social

Michael Anderle Social
Website:
http://www.lmbpn.com

Email List:
http://lmbpn.com/email/

Facebook Here: https://www. facebook.com/TheKurtherianGambitBooks/

Made in the USA
Las Vegas, NV
20 July 2023

75028858R10177